Schooners

In

Peril

Schooners In Peril

True And Exciting Stories About Tall Ships On The Great Lakes

By James L. Donahue

Thunder Bay Press

Holt, Michigan

Holt, Michigan

Table of Contents:

On The Rocks

The Deep Six

Preface

A ship in the United States Navy is any vessel that cannot be removed from the water and taken aboard another, larger vessel. Webster said a ship was a square rigged sailing vessel large enough to have three or more masts. Most people identify a ship as any large commercial vessel that carries passengers and freight. Great Lakes sailors used their own name for the floating machines they worked and sometimes died on. They called them "boats."

Everything about the Great Lakes marine was uniquely different from the world of ships traversing salt water. For years lake "boats" marked their speed in terms of miles per hour instead of knots. Because the Great Lakes offer a turning, twisting course filled with such obstacles as islands, submerged reefs, narrow rivers, locks and man-made channels linking one lake to another, lake skippers still need the intuitive knowledge of a riverboat pilot to make safe passage.

It should not be surprising that in their hey-day, the sailing vessels of the Great Lakes looked slightly different than the tall ships elsewhere. Marine Engineer Bernard E. Ericson, in a paper published in the summer 1969 edition of *Inland Seas* magazine, noted that "lakers" were distinguished by their square sterns and a mizzen-mast that was shorter than the other two masts. In addition, he said the hull design was "more rakish, with shoal draft hulls fitted with a drop keel or centerboard" which allowed vessels to navigate in shallow restricted waters. The centerboard, by the way, was introduced by the British Navy on Lake Champlain in 1776.

Sailing ships first appeared in the lakes in 1678 when French explorer Robert Caveiler La Salle built four small ten ton sloops to carry supplies from Fort Frontenac on Lake Ontario. The following year La Salle built the famed *Griffon,* believed to have been modeled after the Dutch Galliot, on the headwaters of the Niagara River at the eastern tip of Lake Erie. He planned to use the *Griffon* to explore the lakes, and actually sailed it across Lakes Erie, Huron and into northern Lake Michigan. The *Griffon* was lost in the fall of 1679 with all hands after La Salle sent it on a return trip with a load of furs he bought from the Indians at Green Bay. Its where-abouts remains a mystery.

Tall ships were the only vessels seen on the lakes un-til steamships made their appearance between 1816 and 1818. It has been said that the "golden age" of sailing ships occurred between 1820 and 1880. More than two thousand sailing ships were registered and apparently operating on the lakes in 1870. The building of locks at Sault Ste. Marie and the dredging of deeper and wider waterways linking Lakes Huron, Erie and Ontario allowed for the construction of larger vessels capable of carrying quantities of grain, iron ore, copper, coal and lum-ber from Chicago and Duluth to Detroit, Buffalo and Toronto. It was also during this period that America was inundated with settlers from foreign lands who used the natural water-ways from New York to Chicago to travel west. Railroads were being built, but the best way to travel was still by water. Most of the lucrative passenger trade went to the steamship lines, while the schooners and barks carried freight. Business was good.

Because of the abundance of oak and other hardwood trees, schooners were built at many of the lakeport communi-ties, mostly to handle freight traffic of local interest. Major shipyards sprang up in places like Chicago, Milwaukee, Bay City, Port Huron, Detroit, Cleveland and Buffalo. The design of the lakers evolved to meet the demands of the peculiar and often dangerous conditions of the lakes.

The barkentine seems to have been part of the evolu-tion in ship's rigging. Ericson's article noted that the barkentine type of rigging may have originated on the lakes because it was not seen in Europe until after it was used on larger three masters here. But even the barkentine, or "bark" as it was called by lake sailors, disappeared after about 1870. The masters liked the square sails on the fore mast for taking advantage of down-wind sailing across open waters, but in the long run, they opted to give up speed for safety and economy.

Schooners, then, became the sailing vessel of choice. The triangle-shaped sails, which were raised from a boom that swung close to the deck, could mostly be raised and lowered with the help of ropes and pulleys from below, while square

The barkentine is believed to have first appeared on the Great Lakes. It is distinguished by square sails on the foremast.

rigged ships required sailors to go aloft to take in canvass. Thus the schooners, while slower on a long trip than square rigged vessels, could operate with smaller crews and they could be maneuvered in and out of tight areas with greater ease.

Most of the lake sailing ships were small, ranging from about seventy to one hundred fifty feet in length. They sported two or three masts. After Congress appropriated money to dredge deeper channels in the St. Marys, St. Clair and Detroit Rivers to accomodate heavier and wider draft ships, some of the sailing vessels built after 1870 got large. For examples, the *James Couch,* launched at Port Huron in 1871, measured two hundred and ten feet and sported four masts. The *Olive Jeanette,* built at Bay City in 1890, measured two hundred forty-two feet and also was a four-master. The Canadian schooner *Minnedosa,* launched at Kingston in 1890, was a foot longer than the *Jeanette.* It was believed to have been the largest schooner ever built in Canada. Lastly listed, the *David Dows,* built at Toledo in 1881, measured a whopping two hundred sixty-five feet in length and sported five masts. The *Dows* was the only five masted ship ever built on the lakes and it may have been the only vessel of its kind in the world.

Ship owners discovered that the Great Lakes was not a good place for maneuvering sailing ships measuring more than two hundred feet in length. Even rigged as schooners,

3

these vessels got in trouble. They ran down smaller ships and struck bottom trying to squeeze through narrow channels while heavily laden with grain or iron ore. Within a few years, all of the big sailing ships were stripped of their upper masts and converted for use as tow barges, drawn behind steam powered ships. The concept worked so well that new and larger barges were made. The *Santiago,* built at Bay City, Michigan, in 1899, measured three hundred twenty-four feet. Although classified as a schooner, it was designed as a tow barge and probably never raised its sails to travel from port to port on its own. The masts and sails were there to assist the towing barge and also to bring the vessel into port in the event of an emergency.

The Civil War, from 1861-1865, had a long-lasting effect on marine activities on the Great Lakes. Many of the finest vessels, mostly steamships, were siezed by the government and placed in service on either the Atlantic or the Mississippi River. Older, worn-out ships remained on the lakes, as did sailors who were either too old or too handicapped to serve in the Union Army. Thus the vessels plying the lakes during and immediately following the war were aged, many of them long overdue for retirement. They were operated by old men, women and children. Storms, naturally, took terrible tolls in both lives and ships during that period.

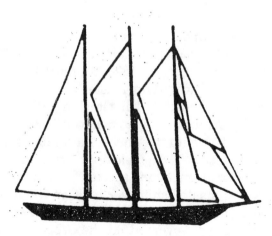

The three-masted schooner was a familiar sight on the lakes before the turn of the century.

One oddity that grew from human ingenuity during the war was the invention of lumber rafts. A lack of vessels to carry lumber from the many camps led to increased shipping costs, so shippers developed a way to make giant square rafts out of the logs. The rafts were cribs made of poles usually measuring about forty feet square. One tug could pull a long line of rafts from the lumber camps to the mills, many located on Lake Erie. The tug boat skippers eventually started to compete in the size of raft their boats were capable of pulling. In July, 1873, the tug *Relief* pulled two giant rafts from Saginaw Bay to Tonawanda, New York, containing two and one-half million feet of lumber. The rafts contained two hundred and fifty cribs covering an estimated twelve acres. It may have been the record.

Nearly all of the sailing ships on the lakes were made of wood. Wooden ships generally were worn out after about thirty years of service. Some wooden sailing vessels continued faithful duty for fifty to sixty years, but they owed their longevity to careful maintenance by their owners, including complete rebuilding and replacement of decaying timbers from time-to-time.

Because there were so many wooden sailing ships operating on the lakes before the turn of the century, vessel accidents were as common then as automobile accidents are on American roads today. Daily newspapers carried lists of mishaps involving lake vessels on a marine page. Of course, reports about the more serious accidents ended up as they do today, on page one. This book is a collection of stories about things that happened to the tall ships.

Capsized

The experience of being trapped below deck in a capsized ship is limited by our own imaginations. Survivors of such accidents at sea were more the exception than the rule during the years of sailing ships. Most of the time when it happened, others could only speculate on what it might have been like to be in a flooded, darkened world where everything was upside down. Escape defied logic because getting out meant to swim downward, through a winding, twisting maze of passageways, doors and steps, until reaching the main deck. Terrified victims of such a disaster most often died because they failed to think clearly. In their confusion they swam upward, toward the bottom of the overturned ship, where there could be no escape.

*The **Hunter Savidge** killed four passengers when it capsized on Lake Huron. Courtesy Institute for Great Lakes Research*

An Unexpected Death
On a Summer Afternoon

*The following is a fictitious account about events surrounding the tragedy of the **Hunter Savidge**, a schooner lost in Lake Huron in 1899. The facts are correct. Possible events and conversations were added by the author to enhance historical understanding.*

The freshly painted ship stood tall and stark against the intense heat of the day, its canvass hanging slack from the two towering masts. The date was Sunday, August 20, 1899, and the schooner *Hunter Savidge* lay becalmed in the middle of Lake Huron. There hadn't been a ripple in those sails or the lake since mid-morning. Now, as the afternoon wore on, Capt. Fred Sharpstein was working off his growing impatience by pacing the deck. His clothes were drenched from perspiration but he continued his pacing, his right fist clenched.

"It is not going to help," a woman's voice said. "But maybe if you run around fast enough you can generate some wind," she giggled.

"Very funny," the captain snapped in recognition that his wife, Rosa, had just joined him on the quarter deck. He stopped his pacing to receive her gift of a fresh apple, taken aboard during the stop the previous day at Sarnia, Ontario, where the *Savidge* unloaded a cargo of coal. "I guess I am making a fool of myself," Sharpstein conceded as the two of them leaned together over the side rail, looking out over the mirror-flat water of the lake. "It is almost four o'clock. I suspect the wind will pick up in a few hours, when the sun gets lower. We will probably get some offshore breezes. I expect to be home in Alpena sometime tomorrow."

As they stood, quietly enjoying each other's company, Sharpstein slowly ate his apple as he peered off into the afternoon's haze, trying to get a glimpse of the Michigan shoreline that he knew was only a few miles away. It was no use, the air was thick with fog created by the hot and very humid air hanging heavily over the cooler lake water. As the day wore on the fog seemed to be thickening. While it offered some protection from the hot rays of the summer sun, the captain worried that the *Savidge* was nearly hidden from approaching steam ships. If it gets any thicker we will have to start sounding fog signals, he thought.

A child's laughter interrupted his thoughts. He looked around to see Mary Mullerweiss and her six-year-old daughter, Etta, walking across the open deck to join them. Mrs. Mullerweiss, the wife of the ship's owner, Alpena businessman John Mullerweiss, and Rosa Sharpstein were on the last leg of a week-long vacation voyage to Cleveland.

"It's so hot, I worry about the men below," Mary said. "I don't know how they can stand it down there." She was talking about the sailors Sharpstein had sent below to scrub the coal dust out of the empty hold. Among them was the Sharpstein's sixteen-year-old son, John, a twin, who was exploring the possibility of following his father's footsteps to a life on the lake boats. Sharpstein knew that it was a hot and dirty job. Most jobs aboard ship were like that. The captain saw no difference between scrubbing the hold while docked in port or doing the work while standing becalmed in the middle of the lake. It was a job best done while the ship was not rolling. Getting the hold cleaned now would save hours of time after the *Savidge* made port. Sharpstein resented Mary Mullerweiss' intercession in the matter, but she was the wife of the man he worked for. He wisely buttoned his thoughts.

"Perhaps you are right," he said after an awkward moment of silence. He called to the mate, Thomas Duby, whom he noticed standing near the binnacle and told him to order the workers out of the hold. "Tell them to clean up and get ready for their regular watches. I expect we will be getting some wind again soon."

"None too soon for me," answered the stalwart Duby. "This standing around in the middle of nowhere is getting on my nerves."

Even as he heard the commotion of the men climbing the wooden ladders to the deck, Sharpstein sensed a change in the weather. The fog covered it, but somehow there was a darkening of the western sky and he felt a touch of new air against his face. He didn't understand why the sensation gave him a chill. "Something's coming," he shouted at Duby. "Have the men ready to get underway again."

"Aye," came the mate's dutiful reply. Orders were snapped. Sailors were on the deck. Motion everywhere.

The sky darkened quickly and the captain realized that a storm was building. He looked up at the yards of canvass hanging overhead. Every sail was hung in the hope of catching the faintest breeze. A shiver raced down his spine. Of course! A summer squall! There would be wind. He realized the danger. "Get those sails reefed. Snap to it now!" he heard himself shouting, knowing that even as he gave the order it was too late. He heard the wind and the fury now. Great danger was but a mile away and racing across the water toward the ship.

"What is happening?" asked Rosa, who still stood by the captain's side.

"It's a squall," he said. "You and Mary and Etta must get below and out of the storm. Things could get ugly up here in another minute."

His last vision of the women was watching them rush toward the steps that led down to the after cabin. Sharpstein stood anxiously near the wheel, waiting for the blast to strike, watching the crew around him race against time to get the sails pulled down. Everything seemed to be moving in slow motion. The roar got louder and louder. When it struck, the blast nearly knocked him off his feet. Overhead the sails filled with the wind that struck the idle ship broadside. He heard a loud cracking noise as the masts strained to take the wind. Then, to his horror, the ship tilted before the wind, then rolled on its starboard side. Sharpstein felt himself falling then sinking in water. He wasn't sure where the air stopped and the water started. He couldn't breathe. He kicked his arms and legs and eventually returned to the surface. There was a roaring sound in his ears as the storm raged overhead. Around him he sensed many struggling bodies. The *Savidge* was turned completely upside down. The ship's wooden hull was high out of the water and the sailors swam for it.

Sharpstein would have nightmares for the rest of his life about the accident and the terrible minutes that followed. He saw his son, John, only briefly. The youth was clinging to a ladder with one hand and grasping wildly with the other, perhaps in an effort to reach his father. Then the boy disappeared, drawn down by the heavy boots he still wore from scrubbing the ship's hold. Sharpstein was only a few feet away but he couldn't reach his son in time. John was never seen again.

His grief was so overwhelming that Sharpstein had difficulty drawing up to the capsized wreck to save himself. The other sailors pulled him in, making him do what was necessary. The captain remembered the women. . . knew they were still in the cabin inside the overturned ship. Perhaps an ax. Anything to claw his way through the oak and get to them. But there was nothing for him to do. He put his ear to the hull and heard strange noises. Pieces of the ship pulling apart, or perhaps water rushing into the hull. Who knows the sounds a ship makes while sinking. Sharpstein later told friends that he believed he heard tapping noises made by someone still alive inside the hull.

Out of the water rose Charles Cook, the ship's steward, gasping for breath. "I was below," he announced. "But I got out through a port hole. I thought I was a goner, for sure!"

"The women? What of the women?"

Cook said he saw nothing of the women. He said that

when the ship went over, he kept his wits and swam his way through the darkness until he came to the port hole, found it open, and slipped through.

It seemed as if they had been in the water for a long time, but in reality it had only been about twenty minutes when the steamer *Alex McVittie* came upon the overturned schooner and sent a boat to pick up survivors. Taken aboard the *McVittie* with Sharpstein were Cook and sailors George Ellery, Ed Bleeland and Joslin Francis. It was at about this time that Sharpstein realized that his mate, Tom Duby, also was among the missing. Nobody saw Duby go.

Sharpstein was in such a deep state of shock when he went aboard the *McVittie* that he didn't protest when the steamer pulled away, assuming its northerly course. The crew later transferred to the southbound steamer *N. E. Runnels,* which took them to Sand Beach, the old name for Harbor Beach, Michigan. The master of the *McVittie* later came under criticism from the citizens of Alpena for not searching for bodies or trying to tow the schooner. After hearing Sharpstein's story, many agreed that there was a chance the women were still alive in the wreck when the *McVittie* left the scene. The old newspaper accounts did not explain why the captain of the steamer did not try to offer more assistance than he gave.

Captain Sharpstein could only think of one thing after reaching port. He wired Mullerweiss in Alpena, informing him of the accident, and asked that the tug *Frank W.* be sent from Alpena to help search for the wreck. Sharpstein hired the fishing tug *Angler* to take him back out to his capsized ship. He could not rest until he made one last effort to save his beloved Rosa. It was too late. The *Savidge* was never seen again.

No one knows how long it floated before slipping to the bottom. Its location remained a mystery until about 1987 when research diver David Trotter and members of Undersea Research Associates, of Canton, Michigan, found the wreck. Trotter said it lies in about two hundred feet of water somewhere off Grindstone City, at the tip of the Thumb District. Its exact location is a secret. Trotter said he regards the wreck as a tomb, since the bodies of the victims are still inside. For this reason, and because he objects to the scavenging of wrecks by some sport divers, he said he will not tell its location.

Trotter said the *Hunter Savidge* apparently went over on its starboard side because a two-hundred-foot long chain slipped out of its locker on that side of the vessel. One end of the chain dropped to the bottom of the lake while the wreck was still afloat. Trotter believes the ship slid under while on a forty-five degree angle, and it was still tilted on that angle when it hit the bottom. The impact split the ship's bow, broke up the hull, and snapped off both masts about two or three feet above the deck. The wreck lies in pieces on the lake floor. "I never expected to find her broken up like that. She was sailing light and wasn't put down by a storm. I always thought if we found the *Hunter Savidge,* she would be intact."

The *Hunter Savidge* measured one hundred and seventeen feet in length. It was built twenty years earlier, in 1879, at Grand Haven, Michigan.

Sources:
　　Blade-Crescent, Sebewaing, Mich., "The Schooner *Hunter Savidge* Discovered Off Pt. Aux Barques," Nov. 8, 1988.
　　Harbor Beach Times, Captain Fred Sharpstein's personal account of the wreck, Aug. 25, 1899, from bound newspaper file in Harbor Beach clerk's office, Harbor Beach, Mich.
　　Notes from interview with David Trotter, fall 1988, in author's possession.
　　Trotter, David, "Shattered Dreams; The *Hunter Savidge* Story," *Diving Times,* Winter 1988-89.
　　Van Der Linden, Rev. Peter, *"Hunter Savidge,"* from Great Lakes Ships We Remember III, Marine Historical Society of Detroit, Freshwater Press, 1994, page 342.

*The **R. P. Mason** killed its master and four other sailors when it capsized on Lake Michigan. Courtesy Institute for Great Lakes Research.*

Saving the *R. P. Mason*

It was October 14, 1871. The three-masted schooner *R. P. Mason* had been hung up on Waugoshance Point in the Straits of Mackinac for six days and the salvage tug *Leviathan* was working against time to save it.

The five-year-old schooner was in big trouble. Bound from Chicago to Detroit with a heavy cargo of grain, flour and meat in its holds, the ship stove an eight-foot-wide hole in its wooden bottom when it struck the rocky reef on October 8. To prepare the *Mason* to be refloated, divers temporarily patched the hole with heavy canvas and then fired two portable steam-powered pumps mounted on the deck. While the water was getting pumped out of the hold, workers removed most of the cargo.

A lighter, or flat-bottom barge, was tied alongside the stricken ship while tons of material was transferred. The *Mason's* cargo consisted of nine thousand bushels of corn and oats, one hundred and fifty barrels of pork, fifty barrels of beef, one hundred and twenty-five barrels of flour and a variety of other things, all destined for Detroit markets.

After days of hard work, the *Mason* was pulled off the reef late on Saturday afternoon, even as workers had their

15

eyes fixed on thickening clouds to the west. Rapidly falling barometric pressure indicated that a storm was building. The sailors knew they had to make a run for shelter and that the *Mason* wasn't out of danger yet. The *Leviathan* hooked a tow line to the schooner and steamed off that evening toward Little Traverse Bay, about thirty miles to the west.

The storm caught the two ships in the open waters of Sturgeon Bay, off Cross Village. As they met the gale head-on, the *Mason* strained at the tow rope. Before the night was over the schooner broke free, broached in the seas and capsized. The two steam pumps tumbled overboard, their hot fires exploding in a blast of steam. The *Mason's* skipper, Capt. Thomas Phall, crew members E. Martin, Louis Hale and William Beeba, and a man known only as Hanson were drowned. Four other sailors clung to the overturned hull until they were rescued by a small boat from shore.

There were conflicting stories about what caused the accident. Some said the hawser broke. Another story said the tow line got tangled in the *Leviathan's* propeller and the crew was forced to cut the line to save their own ship.

The *Mason* drifted ashore upside down near Cross Village. It appeared to be, by then, a complete wreck. But the schooner wasn't finished. While cabins and spars were wrecked, the hull remained sound. The *Mason* was salvaged again, and this time the salvage was successful. The ship served another forty-six years before fire destroyed it on Lake Michigan in 1917.

Sources:

    Detroit Daily Post, stories from Oct. 23 and Nov. 16 editions, 1871, microfilm rolls, Detroit Public Library.

    Detroit Free Press, clippings from Oct. 21 and Nov. 16, 1871, microfilm rolls, Detroit Public Library.

    Master file on *R. P. Mason,* Institute for Great Lakes Research, Perrysburg, O.

Shifted Stones

On May 1, 1875, the Clemens brothers stood on the bluff at Marblehead, Ohio, and watched the schooner *Consuello* capsize and sink in a Lake Erie gale. They launched a skiff and braved the storm to reach the wreck, which by then was showing only the tip of its masts. It was a long and dangerous haul because the schooner was sunk seven miles off shore. By the time they arrived, they found only two of the seven crew members alive. Fred Donahue, the mate, and sailor James King were clinging to the ropes on the masts. Drowned were Capt. H. M. Hauser, his wife, who was aboard as the ship's cook, and sailors William Clary, Charles Peterson and William Law.

After he was rested, Donahue gave his story to a reporter for the *Cleveland Herald*. He said the *Consuello* left Cleveland at about 1:00 AM that morning with a load of block stone, bound for Toledo. While on the lake the storm developed and as the seas built, he said the schooner began rolling. The large blocks of stone stacked on the deck shifted, causing the *Consuello* to take on a dangerous list. After that the ship could not be steered and it drifted before the wind toward Kelly's Island. As the seas struck it from broadside, the ship rolled wildly. The giant waves threatened to send the listing ship over on its beam ends at any moment.

When close to the island, Captain Hauser ordered the crew forward with an order to drop the anchors. He hoped that by turning the vessel around, with its bow into the wind and seas, the severe rolling motion would stop and the schooner could be saved. The order came too late. With a great rumble the stones began to slide, the ship went over and the sailors found themselves swimming for their lives. Donahue said Hauser and some of the sailors close to him made a last moment dash for the stern in an attempt to launch the life boat, but they were too late. Donahue and King, who were working together near the bow, both grabbed the fore-rigging as the capsized ship filled and sank. They were lucky because the *Consuello* jerked upright the moment it hit bottom, and the two sailors were hoisted back out of the water. They found themselves in the ship's cross trees.

Donahue said that from his vantage point, he watched the other members of the crew drown but could do nothing to save them. He said Peterson was the first of the struggling swimmers to disappear under the waves. Captain Hauser yelled out, and then, with his hands uplifted as if attempting to grab something to hold onto, he went down and was not seen again. Mrs. Hauser also disappeared quickly. The two others found pieces of flotsam and by holding on to it, lasted a little longer before the numbing cold of the water killed them. Donahue said Law caught hold of the overturned yawl, then lost his grip and drowned. Clary was grasping a floating trunk before he died.

Donahue and King hung in the ropes of the wreck for about an hour and a half before help arrived. The salvage tug *Winslow,* which was working near Kelly's Island, arrived at the wreck site shortly after the Clemens Brothers got there. The tug took everybody aboard for a ride back to land.

Source:

    Cleveland Herald, "Loss of the Schooner *Consuello*—Full Particulars," May 4, 1875, news clippings, Institute for Great Lakes Research, Perrysburg, O.

More Shifted Stones

The schooner rigged scow *Mayflower* was heavily laden with sandstone, some of the cargo stacked on the wooden decks in large blocks. The vessel was on a course across Lake Superior, from Houghton to Duluth in tow of the tug *Cora A. Sheldon,* when wind, rain and heavy seas developed off the Keweenaw Peninsula. It was not a serious storm and both the *Sheldon* and the two-year-old *Mayflower* were weathering it well. Captain Bourassa, master of the tug, said he never thought of taking the scow back into the Portage Ship Canal to escape trouble. Instead, the two ships continued on their westerly course toward Duluth.

The *Mayflower* never leaked. The hull stood up to the

rigors of the storm that early June day in 1891. But the ship sank just the same. After traveling about five miles, Captain Bourassa and the crew of the *Mayflower* was confronted that afternoon by the unthinkable . . . a shifting cargo. When some of the giant stones on the deck broke loose and slid a few feet off center, the scow listed. Then as the boulders continued to slide, the ship capsized, turning completely upside down. Fifteen minutes later the *Mayflower* sank.

The cook, Edward Elliott of Mancelona, Michigan, said the accident happened at about 4:30 PM. He said he had just gone on deck to help the crew pull on the foresail. "The *Mayflower* had a heavy deck load of stone and I saw one big block right amidships move about three feet to port; then I saw another block just in front of the after cabin move about a foot." Elliott said he told Capt. Theodore Zerbot what was happening.

The captain ordered crew member Pat Smith "to run aft and stand by the davy (davit) falls and be ready to lower the yawl boat. I guess the bulwarks were busted. Pat went aft and the captain and I followed. The captain took out his knife and cut the bow fall. Just as we got to the stern the *Mayflower* went over to port. I jumped on her starboard rail and just as she went clear over, jumped for the bow of the yawl boat but missed it. Then I sank and I guess I went down about fifteen feet. I thought I never was coming up. When I reached the surface I threw my arm around a bit of floating wreckage. Pat was hanging on to some wreckage and Joe (wheelsman Joseph Roe) was on the bottom of the *Mayflower,* which was floating bottom side up. The captain was swimming about thirty or forty feet away. I saw him quite plainly. He shouted twice 'It's no use, I'm gone!' Then he sank."

William F. Thompson, engineer of the tug, said as soon as the *Mayflower* started over, Captain Bourassa ordered the tow line cut and then he turned around to rescue the crew. "We picked up three men. I didn't see a sign of Captain Zerbot, although at first I thought I did, but it proved to the a hat of one of the other men." There were only four crew members aboard the scow and all were rescued except Zerbot.

Thompson said the scow sank in deep water and blew itself apart as it dropped. "A few minutes after the *Mayflower* went down her forward house, after cabin, hatch covers, spars and a lot of other wreckage came up. I think she is pretty well broken up."

Source:
        Detroit Free Press, "A Life Lost at Duluth," June 3, 1891, microfilm rolls, Library of Michigan, Lansing, Mich.
        Duluth Daily News, "Sunk in the Lake, June 3, 1891, news clipping, Institute for Great Lakes Research, Perrysburg, O.

Trapped

The small schooner *Kitty Grant* killed its entire crew of four when it capsized in a storm on Lake Michigan on the night of October 7, 1884. Critics said the vessel's deck was so heavily loaded with wooden shingles that the *Grant* was obviously top heavy when it cleared port earlier in the day. The schooner was bound from Pentwater, Michigan, to Chicago, Illinois, when the storm struck. The next day vessels reported passing through miles of floating shingles. Later, sailors on ships entering Milwaukee said they spotted the overturned hull of a schooner a few miles off shore. A tug identified by the *Detroit Free Press* as the *Getty,* reportedly found the overturned wreck adrift off Muskegon on about October 12. The tug made an unsuccessful attempt to tow it into port. That may have been the last time it was seen. The *Grant* was never recovered.

Killed were Capt. Daniel Davis, and crew members John Cook, Warren Cook and Fred Haightby. All were believed to have lived in Saugatuck, Michigan. Captain Davis owned the 30-year-old schooner.

Source:
        Beers, J. H. & Co., Chicago, Ill., "History of the Great Lakes Illustrated, Volume I, 1899. Chapter XL, p 741.
        Cleveland Herald, "Marine Record," Oct. 14, 1884, news clipping, Institute for Great Lakes Research, Perrysburg, O.
        Detroit Free Press, "The *Kitty Grant* Found and Her Crew Lost," Oct. 14, 1884, microfilm rolls, Library of Michigan, Lansing, Mich.
        Morning News, Muskegon, Mich., "A Wrecked Vessel," Oct. 12, 1884, microfilm rolls, Library of Michigan, Lansing, Mich.

*Schooner **Garibaldi** under full sail during happier times. Courtesy Institute for Great Lakes Research.*

Waterlogged, Tipped and Adrift

Spring gave the appearance of early arrival in 1880, and lake captains were quick to take advantage of it. That was why a lot of vessels were caught on Lakes Michigan and Huron during a series of late winter gales and blinding snow storms in mid-April. Among them was the two-masted schooner *Garibaldi,* whose master was a Captain Peterson of Muskegon, Michigan. The seventy-eight foot long schooner was sailing southwest across Lake Michigan from Muskegon to Milwaukee with lumber both in the hold and lashed on the deck. Peterson's only help was his nephew, Carl Jorgensen, serving as a deck hand.

The wind was growing in power on Friday, April 16, but the *Garibaldi* seemed to be weathering it well. At about 3:00 PM Peterson told Jorgensen to stand at the wheel while he reefed the topsail. While at that task the wind suddenly shifted and countered the boom, sweeping Peterson overboard. Jorgensen stood aghast for one long terrible moment. He couldn't believe what had just happened. He realized that if his uncle had a chance it was going to be up to him to act, and act quickly. But what to do? Jorgensen had some experience handling sailing ships, but he was still a novice. He didn't know the danger involved in attempting to turn a sailing ship around in the midst of a strong wind. Minutes after he turned the wheel, the *Garibaldi* broached, then tipped on its side. The young sailor found himself swimming in a cold and angry sea. He managed to reach the overturned ship and hang on. That saved his life. In a few minutes, the ship's foremast broke from the strain and the *Garibaldi* righted again, bringing Jorgensen back up on the deck again.

The boy was out of the sea, but still in trouble. He was alone on a floating wreck which was being blown about at the mercy of the storm. The forward mast was gone but the sails and rigging were hanging overboard like a big sea anchor, still attached to the schooner. The ship's holds were full of water, but the vessel remained partially afloat because it didn't sink. Both the boat and the cargo were wood. That condition was known as being waterlogged. It only happened during the age of wooden ships. It was a dangerous condition. Many a sailor rode his waterlogged craft in those years until help came or he perished from exposure.

The *Garibaldi* apparently had no lifeboat because Jorgensen didn't try to launch it. Instead he lashed himself to the boat's masthead, shouting and waving at passing vessels. Two ships passed that afternoon but they didn't stop. Then night came and Jorgensen endured terrible loneliness, suffering from cold and extreme hunger while clinging to a storm-tossed wreck in total darkness. He knew that to sleep was to die, so he fought to stay awake. By the next morning he said he had given up all hope and decided to doze off. Death was close. Something marred his stupor, however, and when he looked, Jorgensen saw a ship standing only a few hundred feet off. It was with a great effort that he raised his arm one last time and waived a handkerchief.

Standing on the quarter-deck of the nearby schooner *Belle Mitchell* was Captain Vincent, with his glass trained on Jorgensen. When the hand went up, Vincent said he knew for sure that the man he was watching was still alive. He sent a boat and took Jorgensen aboard, then took the *Garibaldi* in tow to Chicago. The *Garibaldi's* deck load of ten thousand feet of lumber was lost in the storm and there was extensive damage to the ship.

The *Garibaldi* enjoyed many more years on the Great Lakes after that. It was rebuilt at Detroit in 1888 and its enrollment didn't end until 1925. The schooner was built at New Liverpool, Michigan, in 1869.

Sources:

    Chicago Inter Ocean, "Rough Winds Accompanied by Loss of Life," April 19, 1880, news clipping, Institute for Great Lakes Research, Perrysburg, O.

    Master file information on *Garibaldi,* Institute for Great Lakes Research, Perrysburg, O.

Saga of the *City of Toledo*

The *City of Toledo* kept its name, but not its identity during the forty-four memorable years it operated on the Great Lakes. The *Toledo* was built to be a side-wheel steamer at Toledo, Ohio, in 1865. After it was ravaged by a fire at Manistee, Michigan nine years later, the vessel was rebuilt as a schooner. By the time it was destroyed in a freak accident on the Detroit River in 1909, the *Toledo* was stripped down and operating as a tow barge.

This ship's career was marred by three major accidents. In addition to the fire in 1874, the vessel capsized with the loss of all hands on Lake Michigan in 1892, and at the end, was crushed under a drawbridge. Close examination defends the vessel against those who would say it was bad luck that caused the *Toledo's* troubles. Everything that happened was brought on by a combination of human error and foolishness.

The August 24, 1874 fire started in a pile of slab wood piled too close to the boilers in the engine room. The ship had been moored at the foot of Oak Street at Manistee that Sunday morning to take on a cargo of thirty cords of dry pine slabs. The ship was scheduled to take on passengers and leave for Muskegon, Michigan, at four o'clock. By 3:00 PM the lumber was packed in the holds and even stacked on the enclosed main deck. Then fingers of flame were seen dancing through an opening on the upper deck around the walking beam. Within moments, dense volumes of thick black smoke rose from cracks beside the smoke stack. Someone in the pilot house pulled the ship's steam whistle to sound the alarm. Two steam powered fire engines were summoned as were the harbor tugs *Getty, Williams, Edwards, Stevens, Parsons* and *Osgood.* Unfortunately, the fire had gotten a good start in the cargo. By the time it was extinguished eight hours later, the *City of Toledo* was a ruined, burned-out wreck. There were no passengers on the *Toledo* when the fire started so casualties were few. One local fire fighter was overcome by heat and smoke.

The *Chicago Inter Ocean* described the scene in its August 26 edition: "Above deck the steamer's cabin, from the passenger stairs, which are situated about amidships, forward, is ruined; the staterooms on the port side being burned out, and those on the starboard side badly charred. The beams supporting the promenade deck are also either entirely burned away or so badly charred as to be unfit for further service. The cabin and stateroom furniture, bedding, etc., were all removed from the steamer, but badly damaged in handling. A steam pump cleared the steamer's hold of water by last evening, when an inspection showed that the main deck, from the after side of the gallows frame forward to the bow, is nearly burnt through, while the main deck beams are also either destroyed or so badly charred as to be worthless. The wheel beam on the port side is also destroyed. Four upper strakes of ceiling on the port side are burned through, and the tops of the frames are also burned. The hold is filled with the charred remains of piles of slabs and nothing further in regard to the extent of the damage can be ascertained until everything is removed."

The story said the engines were found to be only slightly damaged. The Engleman Transportation Company, which owned the wreck, collected a twenty thousand dollar insurance claim. The *Toledo* was sold to the underwriters, who sold the hull to a Milwaukee salvager. The new owner removed the engines and paddle wheels, repaired the hull and rebuilt the vessel as a schooner. At one hundred and sixty-one feet in length, it was large enough to support a three masts. This was probably its profile when the second disaster came on August 30, 1892.

City of Toledo at about 1904 after conversion as a tow barge. Courtesy Institute for Great Lakes Research

The *Toledo* was owned that year by the Manistee Lumber Company in Manistee, Michigan. Its master was Capt. John McMillan, a resident of Manistee, whose error in judgment cost him not only his own life but the lives of his crew, including his eighteen-year-old daughter, Lizzie, who was aboard as the ship's cook. It was said McMillan ignored the warnings of a tugboat pilot who pulled the *Toledo* out of Manistee harbor at about noon. McMillan told the tugboat skipper he saw two other schooners go out that morning. If they could stand it, he said he guessed he could too.

They said he sailed into the teeth of a building storm with his ship grossly overloaded with thirty-five thousand feet of heavy green lumber, bound for Chicago. Two-thirds of the lumber was piled high on the schooner's decks. The ship was riding so low in the water that only five inches of sideboard was visible above the water line. A sixteen-mile-per-hour wind was kicking up rollers from the southwest and the weather looked threatening.

The schooner barely cleared the harbor before the storm intensified. People watched from shore as the *Toledo* battled the wind, making little progress. The sails were still visible to the men at the Manistee life saving station at 4:00 PM when the winds increased to twenty-one miles per hour. It was about then that McMillan turned his ship back toward

shore, apparently steering northeast to Frankfort or to seek
shelter behind Manitou Island. About dark the wind shifted
to the northwest and blew a gale all night and most of the
next day. The *Toledo* capsized sometime during the night.
Some thought McMillan dropped anchor about two miles offshore and that the heavy seas turned the ship over. A lifeboat
may have been launched. Someone said they thought they
saw four men in an open boat around 7:00 PM. An empty boat
later washed ashore. Also killed were Mate George McKinzie
of Grand Haven, sailors William McCarthy, John Larsen and
Angus McNeil, all of Chicago, and Peter Peterson of Manitoba,
Canada.

The wreck drifted ashore, upside down, fourteen miles
north of Manistee near Pierport, Michigan. The *Toledo* was
salvaged again and returned to service as a schooner-barge.
It sailed the lakes for another fourteen years until it got
crushed by a bridge on the Detroit River. The old barge was
loaded with coal and was under tow behind the propeller
James Fiske when the Belle Isle lift bridge was accidentally
lowered on top of it. This final insult occurred on July 21,
1906. The bridge broke off the spars, opened the hull, and
sent the *Toledo* plunging to the bottom of the river off Owen
Park. The crew escaped. The hull was raised because it was
an obstruction but the *City of Toledo* never sailed again.

Sources:
   Chicago Inter Ocean, "The *City of Toledo,*" Aug. 26, 1874, news clipping,
Institute for Great Lakes Research, Perrysburg, OH.
   Detroit Advertiser and Tribune, "*City of Toledo* Fire," Aug. 25, 1874, mi-
crofilm rolls, Library of Michigan, Lansing, Mich.
   Detroit Free Press, "Eight Lives Lost by the Wreck of the *City of Toledo,*"
Sept. 1, 1892, also "The Wrecked Toledo, Sept. 2, 1872, microfilm rolls, Detroit Pub-
lic Library, Detroit, Mich.
   Greenwood, John O., "Schooner-Barge *City of Toledo,*" from Namesakes
1900-1909, Freshwater Press, Inc., Cleveland, 1987.
   Port Huron Daily Times, "Schooner *City of Toledo* Lost on Lake Michigan,"
Sept. 1, 1892, microfilm rolls, *Times Herald* office, Port Huron, Mich.
   Toledo Blade, "Careless Bridgetender," July 24, 1906, news clipping file,
Institute for Great Lakes Research, Perrysburg, OH.

"We Were Deceived!"

Black ominous looking storm clouds had bedeviled the crew of the schooner *C. G. Breed* most of the morning on November 14, 1879 as the grain-laden schooner made its way across Lake Erie on its way to Buffalo. Each time it happened the ship's crew rushed out on deck and took in sail, expecting high winds, but the clouds brought only rain.

"We must have taken in those sails four of five times and found the clouds contained no wind," said sailor David McCallister. When another evil appearing squall bore down on the ship at noon, in the midst of watch change and as crew members were enjoying the lunch hour, the decision was made to leave the sails hoisted. "This time we were deceived," McCallister said. "We were about twenty-five miles below Ronde Eau when the squall struck us. It came from the southward. We saw it coming over the water at a very lively rate and supposed it was rain. We got its entire strength full on the starboard. The schooner careened to the left so her spars stood at an acute angle. I went for her side as the vessel canted over and was lying on her beam ends."

McCallister was one of only three survivors of the ship's crew of eight. He said that while the *Breed* lay on its side, he half swam and half pulled his way into the rigging near the top of the main mast, hoping that if the ship sank, it would right itself and the mast would lift him up out of the chilled autumn water. The *Breed,* indeed, righted itself when it went down, but the top mast McCallister was clinging to snapped off. After he tumbled in the water he said he grabbed two planks and held on. At first there were other sailors struggling with him. "It must have been about 4:00 PM when I found myself alone in the water. There was no sign of the rest of the crew." McCallister hung on and miraculously stayed alive for the rest of that day and the next night. He was rescued when the schooner *Nellie Gardner* found him at 11:10 AM the next morning.

Captain Harry Rose, who also survived, said he was in his cabin at the stern when the ship capsized. As he groped his way toward the deck he said the cabin broke loose and he found himself swimming under it. Rose said he climbed on top of the wreckage, which he rode like a raft. He was still there when the schooner *Abbie S. L. Andrews* took him off at about 8:00 PM that night.

The third survivor was wheelsman Frank Davis, who was clinging to the rigging of one of the *Breed's* masts when the steamer *Milwaukee* saw the wreckage and stopped at about 1:00 AM the next day. Davis said he had just gone on duty and was at the wheel when the squall hit. "There was a good wind and we were sailing under full canvass. When the vessel went over on her side all on board but the cook, who was below, were thrown in the water. Every man clung to the vessel's side and rigging as long as they could, but as the wind blew a gale and the waves rolled high, they were washed away. The captain and two of the crew succeeded in reaching the yawl boat and loosening her aft, but then they were washed away. One of the sailors floated around to where I was, clinging to the rigging, and clutched my wrists. It was with great difficulty that I released myself from his hold, and when I did, he gripped me around the neck. I knew that it would be impossible to save myself and have him clinging to my neck, so I unloosened his grip and he floated off.

"The vessel lay for about twenty minutes on her side. As she sank, she righted. I clung to the main mast, and as she righted, I was lifted out of the water. I remained in this position until rescued by a yawl from the *Milwaukee.*" Davis said that three hours earlier the propeller *Buffalo* stopped and sent a yawl to examine the wreck. The men in the small boat failed to see any sign of life or hear Davis cry out, and they returned to the steamer. The sailors who perished were first mate William Lawrence, second mate James Smith, James Lawlor, John McCloud and the cook, G. Fenton.

The *Breed* was considered a first rate ship at the time it was lost. The vessel was built at Milwaukee in 1862 and had been on the lakes for seventeen years. It was carrying twenty-four thousand bushels of wheat.

Source:
    Detroit Free Press, "Schooner *C. G. Breed* Sunk in Gale on Lake Erie," Nov. 14, 1879, microfilm file, State Library of Michigan, Lansing, Mi.

Ill-fated schooner Azov upbound light, believed on St. Clair River. Courtesy Institute for Great Lakes Research.

Wreck of the *Azov*

Captain John McDonald of Goderich, Ontario, loved his two-masted schooner *Azov,* even though it was a seasoned vessel of forty years when he bought it in 1906. McDonald saw something special in the *Azov.* Enough that he sold the schooner *John G. Kolfage* to pay for the *Azov* and have it rebuilt at Sarnia.

The *Azov* became McDonald's home away from home. His son, Dan, served with him as the member of the crew, and his daughter, Etta, worked as the cook. The schooner was a happy little ship, busy carrying cargo mostly across Lake Huron. The McDonalds painted their vessel white with green trim. All went well for five good years. Then the *Azov* capsized and wrecked in a gale on October 22, 1911. That the McDonalds and three other crew members survived is a tribute to Captain McDonald's seamanship.

The *Azov* left Meldrum Bay on Friday, October 20, with a load of lumber and shingles bound for Chatham, Ontario.

29

The schooner was working its way across the widest point of the lake, off Saginaw Bay, in heavy weather, when the ship's wooden seams opened and it began to leak. McDonald tacked southwest before the wind in an attempt to get the *Azov* to the lee of the Michigan shore and out of the brunt of the storm. He may have been thinking of mooring at Harbor Beach. The crew took turns at the bilge pump, but it was a losing battle. The ship continued flooding. After a while, it waterlogged and became unmanageable.

As the *Azov* dropped lower and lower in the water, the seas began taking their toll. One especially large wave swept the deck, snapping the cable holding the deck load of lumber in place. The load shifted to port, causing the schooner to take on an ominous list. McDonald now believed he would lose the *Azov*. He gave the order to abandon ship. After getting his family aboard the fifteen-foot-long life boat, mate Henry Kemp and sailors W. S. Malle and Norman McIvor also scrambled in. They hardly got away before the schooner broached, there was a loud cracking sound and the ship rolled on its port side. After that, the sailors didn't see it again. They were within about twenty miles of the Michigan coast, off Point aux Barques, but the strong northwest wind was blowing the boat back out into the lake. Instead of trying to row against the wind, Captain McDonald hoisted a sail and chose a dangerous "only chance" trip east across the lake toward home.

It was a long cold night. As the boat rolled and tossed in the storm, the six occupants suffered untold hardships. They were cold, wet and hungry as they huddled together for what little warmth they could generate from their own body heat. The physical exhaustion and cold brought on a deadly drowsiness. Captain McDonald used his ore as a prod to keep everybody awake. His seamanship was excellent. Twenty hours later the boat touched land three miles north of Goderich. A farmer gave them shelter and arranged for a stage coach ride into Goderich.

The *Azov* followed the McDonald's across the lake. It was found by the tug *McGaw* about five miles off Kincardine. An attempt was made to tow it into port, but the wreck would not follow in tow. It washed ashore and broke up at McGregor Point, near Port Elgin, Ontario. The remains of the *Azov* were located by a grandson, Bruce McDonald and scuba divers removed an anchor in 1956. The anchor is displayed at the Goderich Marine Museum.

The *Azov* was built at Wellington Square, the old name for Hamilton, Ontario, in 1866. It measured one hundred and eight feet, four inches in length and was rated at one hundred and ninety-five gross tons. The ship operated mostly on Lake Ontario until it was sold to Lambton owners in 1884 and was moved to Georgian Bay.

Sources:

Detroit Free Press, "Schooner *Azov* Is Lost in Gale," October 25, 1911, news clips, Institute for Great Lakes Research, Perrysburg, O.

Kohl, Cris, "Worth Checking Out?: The Wreck of the *Azov*," from Dive Ontario, a guide to shipwrecks and scuba diving in Ontario, self published, 1990.

McDonald, Bruce, family story of the wreck of the *Azov*, *Telescope* Magazine, October 1956 edition, Burton Historical Collection, Detroit Public Library.

Van Der Linden, Rev. Peter, *Azov*, from Great Lakes Ships We Remember III, Marine Historical Society of Detroit, Freshwater Press, 1994.

Within Sight of Home

Through the mist and spray of the raging gale, people living and working near the tip of Nine Island Point, at the eastern end of Lake Ontario, watched in horror on the morning of May 11, 1890 as the image of the large three-masted schooner *Jessie L. Breck* loomed into view. Clearly battered by the storm, the *Breck's* sails were torn or reefed and sailors could be clearly seen sweating over the bilge pump, obviously battling to keep the leaking ship afloat long enough to reach a safe haven to the lee of nearby Wolfe Island. One watcher said that after rounding the head of Simcoe Island, the *Breck* became unsteady, lurched from the force of the gale, then disappeared unexpectedly from his view.

Mrs. Dunlop, wife of the lighthouse keeper on Simcoe Island, had a ringside seat to the drama. She said she saw the schooner capsize, then float on its port side as the seas continued to hammer at the wreck and constantly bury the half-drowned sailors who clung to it. She said she watched for about forty-five terrible minutes as the sailors perished before her eyes. Four men hung on the port ratlines and one took to the rigging, but they couldn't hold up against the constant beating of the waves. As their strength wore away, they dropped one-by-one to their deaths. The last man on the bobbing spar stood the longest, Mrs. Dunlop said. He waved his hat continuously, but those who saw him lacked the means to go to his rescue. By the time the tug *Hiram Calvin* reached the scene from Kingston, Ontario, he was also gone. There were no survivors.

Killed were four members of one local family, and a father and son from a second. The dead included Captain Thomas Mackie, his brothers, first mate Joseph Mackie and W. Mackie, and their sister Mary Mackie, who served as the ship's cook. Also lost were William and John Muller, father and son. All had homes and families on Wolfe Island. The other dead crew members were identified as James Davidson, also of Wolfe Island, and Frank George of Kingston.

It was the *Breck's* first trip of the season, and Captain Mackie's first trip of his first command. He had served as first mate on the *Breck* and had been promoted to the rank of the ship's master that spring. The schooner sailed from Kingston four weeks earlier with a cargo of ice, bound for Toledo, and was returning with oak timber from Garden Island.

The wreck continued to float after the storm abated and it was towed into Kingston. It was so extensively damaged that it was never repaired.

Sources:

    Chicago Inter Ocean, "Eight Lives Lost," May 18, 1890, and "The *Breck* Horror," May 19, 1890, news clippings, Institute for Great Lakes Research, Perrysburg, O.

    Detroit Free Press, "Seven Sailors Drowned," May 18, and "The Loss of the *Jessie H. Breck,*" May 19, 1890, news clippings, Institute for Great Lakes Research, Perrysburg, O.

    Duluth Daily Tribune, "Eight Lives Lost," May 18, 1890, news clippings, Institute for Great Lakes Research, Perrysburg, O.

Collisions

Unless you have been there, it is difficult to imagine the effect of two ships in collision. The crash of a sailing ship was unusually messy. Not only was the striking of the hulls a bone-jarring experience for the sailors, but the falling sails, spars, rigging and pulleys threatened the lives of anybody caught on the open deck. Most often the vessel hit from the side was sunk. Sometimes both boats were lost. This was especially true during the days of wooden ships before collision bulkheads were thought of.

Dangerous Pointe aux Barques

Michigan's lower half is, in reality, two peninsula's. Examine the state on a map and the entire lower half looks something like a child's wool mitten. Huron County lies at the tip of what would be the part of the mitten that protects the thumb so people in that territory like to say they live in the "Thumb District." Surrounding the Thumb District are Lake Huron on the north and east and Saginaw Bay on the west. Ships plying Lake Huron usually follow a busy route of vessels passing between Port Huron north toward the Straits of Mackinaw on their way to Chicago, or north around the end of Manitoulin Island on their way through the Sault Ste. Marie locks to Duluth. Another active route might take them around the tip of the Thumb and through Saginaw Bay on their way to Bay City and the Saginaw River. In the early days, before there was radio, radar or even electric lights to help them find their way, the busy crisscrossing string of vessels occasionally collided near the barren, rocky coast that marks the extreme northerly tip of the Thumb. This desolate appearing place is known as Pointe aux Barques. Marine historians believe the place is a rich graveyard of sunken ships, although because of the depth of the water, few have been found. The following are but a few of the stories.

Close Hauled and In Danger

It took great skill to be the master of a sailing ship on the Great Lakes. Unlike the ocean, vessels go through a series of several important turns as they pass through a maze of streams, lakes and channels, then avoid islands, sunken reefs and even occasional rock formations that jut up like daggers from the lake floor in unexpected places. Lake sailors preferred the versatile schooner because its triangular sails could be raised and lowered from the deck without sending a lot of men aloft. Also the vessel's design proved to be more maneuverable than square riggers. Yet even the handy schooners were subject to the whims of the winds. Steamers, on the other hand, lumbered along in any direction its pilot chose to steer, in spite of wind and wave. For this reason, steamboat captains were expected to steer clear of sailing ships when they met. Not just because it was the rule of the road. It was something called courtesy.

Occasionally steamboat masters ignored the sails of nearby ships, or the officer of the deck misjudged the ability of the schooner to get out of the way of the charging steamer. The result was a collision that usually sent the smaller sailing ship to the bottom. Such was the story of the schooner *Dunderburg*, which lies among the bones in the Pointe aux Barques graveyard. The *Dunderburg* was crushed in a collision with the steamer *Empire State* on the night of August 13, 1868.

The *Dunderburg*, under the command of Captain Charles Green, was a new vessel, hardly more than a year old. It was making its way from Chicago to Buffalo with a load of corn and six passengers. The summer night was balmy and there was a light breeze blowing. Both ships were well lighted as they approached one another at about 11:00 PM. The officers of the *Dunderburg* were on deck and aware of the approaching steamer, but the wheelsman said he couldn't steer out of the way because the ship's sails were close hauled, or tacking into the wind. Everybody expected the steamer to make the turn, but it didn't. That call should have come from the *Empire State's* second mate, John Langley, who was standing watch in the wheelhouse. But Langley was not experienced in the ways of sailing ships and he did not realize the schooner off his bow was unable to turn from harms way.

Also on the *Dunderburg's* deck that night were the six passengers, who, like the members of the crew, were enjoying the pleasure of a quiet summer evening on a lake boat. They were Mr. and Mrs. George Fairbrother, Mrs. O. Wilcox, Mrs. Harriet Larzellier and Mrs. E. Goddard, all of Detroit. The passengers and crew members stood watching the approaching steamer, totally unaware of the danger until the two vessels got so close it was obvious they were on a collision course. "People began yelling at the wheelsman to steer off but it was too late," one unidentified survivor said. Captain Green ordered all of the passengers out of the cabin and on the deck moments before the two ships hit. Then came the crash. Both ships crunched to a stop in mid-lake. The *Dunderburg* was not a small ship, at one hundred and eighty-six feet, and it might have held its own against the steamer, but the *Empire State's* bow struck the schooner amidships, cutting a fatal gash in the schooner's wooden hull. Falling ropes, sails and masts added to the terror. All of the lamps on the ill-fated schooner were knocked so hard they went out. The sudden darkness added to the confusion of the moment. People were yelling as they fumbled around in the dark, looking for loved ones, personal belongings and life preservers.

The women passengers were rounded up and put in one of the life boats. It was then that friends realized that Mrs. Wilcox, wife of one of the ship's owners, was missing. She was last seen standing near the rail just before the crash. She had obviously been knocked overboard. Both life boats were launched, and sailors spent the night searching the water for Mrs. Wilcox. She was not to be found. After the schooner sank, the survivors boarded the *Empire State* and the ship steamed south to Port Huron. The steamer was leaking and a steam pump was required after it reached Port Huron to keep the vessel afloat.

Langley was jailed on a charge of manslaughter on the high seas. The charge later was dropped, but a Detroit inspection board voted to revoke Langley's pilot's license.

The *Dunderburg* rests upright on the lake bottom in one hundred and fifty-five feet of water. Divers know the wreck from the unique scroll work and an animal head figurehead still attached under the bow sprit. Because of the depth at which it lies, only experienced divers visit this wreck.

Sources:
    Advertiser and Tribune, Detroit, "Marine Disaster," Aug. 15, 1868, microfilm rolls, State Library of Michigan, Lansing, Mich.
    Detroit Free Press, "Another Lake Disaster," and "The *Dunderburg* Disaster," Aug. 15 and 16, 1868, microfilm rolls, State Library of Michigan, Lansing, Mich.
    Notes from talks with diver David L. Trotter, director of Undersea Research Associates, who has visited and photographed the *Dunderburg.*
    Toledo Blade, "Propeller Seized," "The *Dunderburg* Disaster," and "License Revoked," Aug. 19 and 31 and Sept. 9, 1868, news clippings, Institute for Great Lakes Research, Perrysburg, O.

Too Busy to be Bothered

Capt. George McMinn Jr., master of the crack Lehigh Valley Line steamer *Clyde*, wasn't pleased about the news that his ship was in collision with one of the hundreds of coastal schooners at work on the Great Lakes. At age forty-one, McMinn was enjoying the self-proclaimed importance of his fourth year of command. Even though he was a new skipper, he already was assigned to a steamer in one of the best shipping lines in the business. The Lehigh Line was in the business of fast-hauling freight between Buffalo and Chicago, important ports located at both ends of the lakes.

There was no excuse for the collision. The *Clyde* bore down on the schooner *Arctic* off Lake Huron's Pointe aux Barques in crisp clear weather, in broad daylight, on September 17, 1895. The crew of the little sailing ship saw the steamer coming, but by the time they realized it was not going to change course, they couldn't get out of its way or do anything to avoid the impending crash. Sailor George Crittenden of Milwaukee, from the *Arctic's* crew, blamed McMinn for sending the

*Schooner **Arctic** is one of a fleet of vessels lying sunk near Lake Huron's Pointe aux Barques. Courtesy Institute for Great Lakes Research.*

Arctic to the bottom. "There was nothing to obstruct the vision," he said. They "have not the slightest excuse for their carelessness." Crittenden and the schooner's skipper, Capt. Antonio Peterson of Grand Haven, said they had the schooner on a starboard tack and couldn't get out of the charging steamer's way. At 9:00 AM the *Clyde* struck the schooner on the port side, just forward of amidships, cutting a six-foot wide gash in the *Arctic's* hull. The steamer never slowed or changed its course even though the sailing ship was in plain view of both the *Clyde's* wheelsman and the lookout.

A story in the *Detroit Free Press* attempted to defend McMinn. The story said McMinn did not stop his ship, "but kept her headway" at about nine miles an hour, which served to lock the wreck of the stricken *Arctic* across the steamer's bow long enough to allow the crew to jump safely to the *Clyde's* deck. All crew members escaped unhurt. It was only after they got aboard that McMinn stopped his ship and backed off, allowing the wreck to sink, the story said. The schooner foundered within ten minutes.

Later, when passing Detroit, McMinn apparently was so concerned about making up the time his ship lost in the collision that he did not dock to drop off the schooner's crew. He put them off on a yawl in the middle of the Detroit River and let them row ashore on their own. The other crew members were Charles Forrest, mate, of Milwaukee; cook Celia Larson of Detroit, and sailors Thomas Evans of Chicago and William Boak of Charlevoix, Michigan.

The *Arctic* was traveling empty from Detroit to Rogers City for a cargo of lumber. The schooner was built in 1853 in Ashtabula, Ohio. It measured one hundred twelve feet in length.

Sources:
    Detroit Free Press, "Collision on Lake Huron," Sept. 19, 1895, news clipping, Institute for Great Lakes Research, Perrysburg, O.
    Evening News, Detroit, "Capsized and Sank," Sept. 18, 1895, microfilm rolls, State Library of Michigan, Lansing, Michigan.
    Master file, Institute for Great Lakes Research, Perrysburg, O.

The Strange Case of the *Emma Nielson*

Among the ghost ships off Pointe aux Barques is the graceful schooner *Emma L. Nielson*. Divers able to brave the depths to reach it are sometimes startled to find the ship sitting upright on the bottom, its sails unfurled, and its rigging in place as if the ship were running before the wind. The abnormalities about the *Nielson's* appearance are that its bow is flattened and that fish, not men, pass over the decks.

The *Nielson* went to the bottom after slamming into the side of the steamer *Wyandotte* in heavy fog at 2:00 AM on June 26, 1911. The ship may have set a precedent. Until then, wooden hulled schooners rarely tried to run down steel ships. The way it usually happened was that the steamers accidentally ran down the sailing ships and then came back to pick up survivors.

The *Emma Nielson's* master, Capt. William Young of Port Huron, Michigan, probably didn't think it humorous the day he lost his command. Young and his tiny crew of two other sailors didn't see the *Wyandotte* until it loomed out of the haze and it was too late to change course. The details of this wreck have been lost over the years but there are some assumptions that can be made based on the facts. Because it was foggy, the wind was probably light. Young had a full set of sails unfurled to capture what little breeze there was. He was doing a good job since his craft was moving along at a fast enough speed to crush its bow when it slammed into the side of the steamer.

The *Wyandotte* was downbound from Alpena, Michigan to Detroit with a cargo of limestone. While jolted by the crash, the *Wyandotte* didn't take a dent. The schooner's more fragile bow was cracked open and it began sinking fast. Captain Young and his crew had just enough time to lower the yawl boat from the stern davits. The *Wyandotte* came around and picked them up before continuing on to Port Huron.

The schooner, which was traveling empty, dropped to the bottom of Lake Huron in a level upright position. It still rests there in one hundred and ninety feet of water about eleven miles off shore. The wreck is deep enough that few

40

*The schooner **Emma L. Nielson** under full sail at about the turn of the century. Courtesy Institute for Great Lakes Research.*

sport divers ever visit, and it consequently has remained unmolested. The three-master measured one hundred four feet in length. It was built at Manitowoc, Wisconsin, in 1883 for Capt. Paul Nielson, who named it for his wife.

Sources:

    Detroit Free Press, "*Nielson* is Sunk; Her Crew Saved," June 27, 1911, microfilm rolls, State Library of Michigan, Lansing, Mich.

    Detroit News, "Steamer *Nielson* is Sunk in Collision," June 27, 1911, microfilm rolls, State Library of Michigan, Lansing, Mich.

    Greenwood, John O., "Schooner-Barge *Emma L. Nielson,*" page 500, from Namesakes 1910-1919, Freshwater Press, Cleveland, O., 1986.

    Port Huron Times Herald, "The *Emma Nielson* Sinks," June 26, 1911, microfilm rolls, St. Clair County Library, Port Huron, Mich.

The Cook Stayed to Pack

The cook died with the three and aft schooner *Falmouth* when it crashed into the Buffalo breakwater and sank on November 21, 1880. Even though at least two other sailors warned her of the impending danger, it was said she refused to leave the ship without taking her clothes. When last seen she was sitting on the cabin floor, wrapping items in a blanket. Capt. Thomas Murray and the five other survivors, identified as mate S. Becker and sailors J. F. Scofield, William McMaster, J. Peverson and James Roach, all jumped to the breakwater and then worked their way to shore. They could not explain the cook's behavior. They said they were glad to be alive after a night of terror trying to keep their ship afloat on storm-tossed Lake Erie.

The *Falmouth* left Toledo, Ohio, at noon on Friday, November 19 with over sixteen thousand bushels of wheat bound for Oswego, New York. Captain Murray said the wind picked up while the ship was off Port Stanley, Ontario, on Saturday afternoon, and by 8:00 PM a heavy snow storm was raging. He steered for shelter behind Long Point. Before the schooner reached the lee shore the wind split the foresail and mainsail, then carried away the foreboom and gaff. During the next two hours the seas also swept away the ship's lifeboat, hawser boxes and several lines. The *Falmouth* drifted helplessly past Port Colborne at about 2:00 AM. With the key sails gone, Murray said the crew could not turn the ship against the wind and sail into the port. Instead, all that could be done was let the *Falmouth* race before the wind, steering in the general direction of Buffalo harbor, and pray for a miracle.

For a while it looked as if the *Falmouth* would escape. Whether from dead reckoning or skilled seamanship, the vessel sailed directly to Buffalo. As the lights of the city came in sight at about 4:00 AM, Murray said his hopes rose when he also saw the lights of the tugs *Compound* and *Rambler* steaming out to meet the *Falmouth*. With help, he felt confident that the ship would be out of danger. That was not the case. The schooner's crew found that the freezing spray from the storm had lodged the schooner's heavy hawsers fast to the deck. The tugboat crews yelled that their hawsers also were frozen and unmanageable. All they could do was run a light line from the *Compound* to the *Falmouth*. While trying to attach that line, the two ships collided with such a crash that some sailors were knocked to the deck. Murray said he didn't know how badly the *Falmouth* was damaged. Then, as soon as the *Compound* began to pull, the line parted. After that, everybody watched helplessly as the wind blew the luckless schooner on toward the breakwater and impending disaster. The crew of the *Compound* raced back into the harbor in a last-ditch effort to secure another hawser, but they didn't have enough time.

The *Falmouth* struck the breakwater broadside. The first blow was violent. After that the ship rode the wash back and forth, each wave grinding the ship into kindling. First the foremast fell, then the mainmast came down. The constant pounding and wrenching opened the ship's hull and it filled and sank near the north end of the breakwater in about twenty-five feet of water.

Sources:
        Chicago Inter Ocean, "Schooner *Falmouth* Sunk," and "The Loss of the *Falmouth,*" Nov. 22 and 26, 1880, news clippings, Institute for Great Lakes Research, Perrysburg, O.
        Cleveland Herald, untitled story, Nov. 26, 1880, news clippings, Institute for Great Lakes Research, Perrysburg, O.

"A Bad Job, Mr. Fraser"

John Fraser, first mate on the iron steamer *Brunswick,* took the blame for the early morning crash on Lake Erie that sank his ship and the wooden schooner *Carlingford.* The record shows, however, that Fraser may have been wrongly accused. In his own defense, he said he thought the schooner luffed, or turned across the steamer's bow at the wrong moment. Whoever blundered, the collision led to the deaths of four sailors on November 12, 1881.

The accident should not have happened. It was a clear night. Both crews watched each other's lights as the vessels approached one another near Dunkirk, N.Y. It was difficult for the men on the bridges of the two ships to explain why they crashed. The *Brunswick,* a new ship under the command of Capt. C. Chamberlain, left Buffalo with fifteen hundred tons of coal at 10:00 PM, bound for Duluth. Chamberlain had ordered a course of west by southwest. The *Carlingford,* with Capt. Homer Durant at the helm, was bound for Buffalo with over twenty-six thousand bushels of wheat. The schooner was tacking against a light southeasterly breeze.

Fraser said he saw the *Carlingford's* green light, mounted on the starboard side, which led him to believe the schooner would pass in a northeasterly direction. He said he told the wheelsman to steer to port so the steamer would pass easily at the *Carlingford's* stern. Moments before the crash, Fraser said the schooner turned across the *Brunswick's* bow. He said he was first aware of it when the wheelsman yelled: "Mr. Fraser, the schooner is coming in stays." Fraser said he took evasive action, but it was too late. The *Brunswick* hit the schooner on the port side with a jolt that split the wooden vessel's hull and cracked the steamer's brittle iron shell.

Captain Chamberlain said he left the bridge at midnight, not long before the collision, and was having a smoke in the ship's galley. "I was putting on my boots to go forward where my room was when I felt a jar and immediately heard a signal for the engine to stop and back. I ran forward and found we had collided with a schooner. I said to the mate: 'This is a bad job, Mr. Fraser,' to which he answered 'Yes, sir, it is.' The second mate came on deck and I sent him below to see if we were leaking. He quickly returned and said, 'Captain, we're sinking!'" Chamberlain said he didn't believe the report at first, but ordered the pumps started and turned the ship toward the nearest shore. If the report was true, he wanted to try to let the ship settle in shallow water.

In the meantime, the seven sailors on the *Carlingford* had no doubt that their vessel was dropping toward the bottom of Lake Erie. They worked against time to launch the ship's lifeboat. The schooner sank so quickly that one crew member, Edward Conway, was caught below decks. Ship mates said that he foolishly ran below to save something personal left in his quarters. The rest of the crew pulled for the Canadian shore and arrived the next morning near Dunville, Ontario.

The *Brunswick* didn't get very far before the engine room flooded. Chamberlain also was forced to give the order to abandon ship. His reluctance to get the life boats away sooner cost three other sailors their lives. The boats were being lowered from both the port and starboard davits even as the steamer's bow was under water, its stern was high and the ship was starting its final plunge. The port side boat, containing the two mates and five other sailors, got away all right. The starboard boat, which carried the captain, the two women

*The steamer **Brunswick** was only a few months old when it sank with the schooner **Carlingford** after a collision on Lake Erie in 1881. Four sailors died. Courtesy Institute for Great Lakes Research.*

cooks, and five other sailors, was still attached to the davits when the ship broke in two parts and sank, pulling the lifeboat down with it.

Chamberlain, who survived the incident, described what happened during those last terrifying moments: "As the steamer sank she seemed to break in two. She took a sudden lurch to the starboard and rolled over the yawl. Mr. (John) Francomb, the engineer, who was on deck shoving the yawl out, seemed to get jammed between her cabin and I never saw him again. I let loose the stern (end) of the yawl but the man at the bow didn't unhook his end, so the yawl was taken down with the steamer. I thought the yawl could come up again and told the cooks to hang to their seats. They did. I never saw them again. I went down a great distance before I let go and I thought I would never get to the top again."

Chamberlain said he and the other men who spilled from the lost life boat clung to floating wreckage until they were picked up by the other boat. The crew then rowed south toward the American shore, arriving near Dunkirk. The lost cooks were identified as Mrs. A. G. Fletcher and her daughter, Millie, both of Detroit.

Sources:
    Beers, J. H. & Co., "Fatal Collision, 1881," History of the Great Lakes with Illustrations, Volume I, Chicago, 1899, page 736.
    Chicago Inter Ocean, "The Loss of the Brunswick," Nov. 15, 1881, news clipping, Institute for Great Lakes Research, Perrysburg, O.
    Cleveland Herald, "Dire Disaster! Collision of Two Vessels on Lake Erie," and "The Sad Story of the Collision on Lake Erie Between the Steamer Brunswick and Schooner Carlingford," Nov. 14 and 15, 1881, news clipping, Institute for Great Lakes Research, Perrysburg, O.

The *Clayton Belle* Mystery

When divers discovered the wreck of the lost schooner *Clayton Belle* in Lake Huron in 1993, they also came upon a century-old mystery. They said they were perplexed at first why the hull was split from stem to stern, with the port side of the ship lying about twelve hundred feet away from the rest of the wreck. "The hull is separated. The deck is gone,

*The **Thomas Parsons** collided with and sank the schooner **Clayton Belle** in lower Lake Huron in 1882. Courtesy Institute for Great Lakes Research.*

and the ship is stripped of anything of any value," said diver Paul Schmitt of Port Huron. One old news story suggested that the ship was severed when the schooner *Thomas Parsons* struck the *Belle's* port bow on the morning of April 12, 1882. "The *Belle* lies in thirty-six feet of water off Lakeport and is in very bad shape," the story in the *Port Huron Daily Times* said. "The *Parsons* struck her on the port bow and that part of the wreck is on top of the water."

Schmitt, an economics professor at St. Clair County Community College, said he doesn't think the impact of the crash could have cut the ship's one hundred and thirty-nine-foot-long oak hull in that way. Instead, he developed a different theory: "The *Belle* was loaded with pig iron. I think they tore it apart to get at the cargo. I can just picture an old steam tug pulling on that hull under full throttle. The schooner was written off as a total loss so to them it didn't matter. "

Capt. Fred A. Colvin and three other members of the *Belle's* crew drowned when the iron-laden ship flooded and foundered less than three minutes after the crash. Also lost were first mate Nathaniel Brotherton, his brother, Dell Brotherton, and the ship's cook, identified only as Mrs. Gifford. Survivor Thomas Irwin said everybody got off the ship before

47

it sank, but then they perished from exposure before the tug *Mocking Bird* stopped to look for survivors an hour later. The second mate, John Dillon, and sailors Charles Chesbro and William Sullivan, escaped by climbing to the deck of the other ship while the two vessels were locked together. All three were asleep in the forecastle, at the bow of the *Belle*. They scrambled from their bunks, climbed to the deck, and find their way to the deck of the *Parsons* before the schooner sank. Irwin said he and the other sailors working near the stern were trapped on the sinking ship. He said he wanted to launch the lifeboat but discovered that the boat was damaged by the ship's falling boom.

The captain of the *Parsons* fell under strong criticism for failing to launch a life boat and search for survivors. Dillon told the *Detroit Free Press* the next day that he and the other men from the *Belle* found the *Parson's* life boat lying on the deck, but out of its davit. He said they tried to launch the boat anyway, knowing that their friends were struggling in the water, but only got help from one of the crew members on the *Parsons*. By the time they got the boat launched, it was too late.

Dillon said the *Clayton Belle* was on a starboard tack, running south, southeast with her sails close hauled against a wind out of the west, southwest. The *Thomas Parsons,* bound northwest, was on a port tack, and could have turned to avoid the accident. The collision happened because the crew of the *Parsons* was reefing sail as the two vessels approached, and a partially hanging sail prevented the *Parsons'* wheelsman from seeing the other ship until it was too late.

A story in a Port Huron newspaper on April 18 said the *Clayton Belle* came to rest upright, with its masts showing out of the water. The sails were still set. It was easy for the Quinn Brothers, a Detroit diving and salvage company, to find the wreck and extricate the five hundred and twenty-two tons of pig iron from its holds. Once the wreck was opened up, a barge was anchored at the site, and the iron was raised in buckets. Schmitt said the salvagers also stripped the schooner. The sails and rigging are gone. So are the iron and brass fittings, the wheel, and even the rudder. The hull, cargo deck, keelson and other parts of the wreck lie in about forty feet of water. The *Belle* was found by Schmitt and divers David Losinski, Roy Young and Tracy Sweet, all of Port Huron. They were aided by a magnetometer, a device that measures changes in the magnetic field on the bottom of the lake. Schmitt said the *Belle* was one of several vessels he had been searching for since 1980.

The *Belle* was traveling from St. Ignace to Erie, Pennsylvania at the time it was lost. The schooner was built in 1868 at Clayton, New York.

Sources:

    Chicago Inter Ocean, "Two Schooners Collide with Fatal Effect in the Waters of Huron," Apr. 13, 1882, news clipping, Institute for Great Lakes Research, Perrysburg, O.

    Evening News, Detroit, "Down to Death," April 12, 1882, microfilm rolls, State Library of Michigan, Lansing, Mich.

    Notes from interview with diver Paul Schmitt in October, 1993, in personal file.

    Port Huron Daily Times, "The Schooner *Clayton Belle* Goes Down on Lake Huron And Four of The Crew Drowned," Apr. 12, 1882; "The *Clayton Belle*," Apr. 13, 1882, microfilm file, State Library of Michigan, Lansing, Mich.

    Detroit Free Press, "Collision on Lake Huron," Apr. 13, 1882, from microfilm file, State Library of Michigan, Lansing, Mich.

The *Sunny Side* Disaster

The horror of what happened was written on the face of Capt. Robert Kerr when he arrived at Detroit on the steam barge *William H. Barnum* on August 22, 1883. "It was a most fearful experience," the fifty-eight-year-old veteran navigator said in describing the collision that sank the bark *Sunny Side.* The vessel was sunk in a summer squall four miles off North Fox Island in northern Lake Michigan three days earlier. It was the only ship Captain Kerr ever lost in his years of command on both the oceans and the Great Lakes. He was visibly shaken. That his wife, Martha, was aboard and almost drowned, made his story even more personal.

He said the bark was one of three ore-laden barges under tow behind the *Barnum*, on their way from Escanaba, Michigan, to Cleveland, Ohio, when the storm struck them at about 9:30 PM. "We took in all our canvas but the foresail and foretopsail. A very heavy squall, accompanied by blinding hail and rain, struck us about 10:30, parting our tow lines." Kerr said the storm quickly generated mountain high seas that thundered across the decks, threatening the lives of the sailors as they struggled to keep the ship afloat. The stormy darkness was so intense that nobody noticed the faint kerosene lamps of the schooner *Samuel H. Foster* as that vessel drifted across the *Sunny Side's* bows. When it was spotted, Kerr said "the *Foster* was so close that a collision was unavoidable, so our wheel was put down so as to strike her at as acute an angle as possible. We struck just abaft the main rigging, which, with the mainmast head, was carried away, also a number of stanchions. Our bowsprit, jibboom and foreyard were carried away. The bowsprit in slewing round, opened up her stem and she commenced to fill."

The broadside collision jarred the *Foster,* toppling the mainmast and doing so much damage the crew thought their ship also was sinking. Everything was in a state of confusion. While the two vessels were briefly locked together, some of the sailors of the *Foster* jumped to the deck of the *Sunny Side*, thinking the *Foster* was going to sink. Later they jumped back aboard the *Foster* as it became evident that the *Sunny Side* would certainly be lost. "The pumps were sounded and the water was found to be over the sounding rod. We made a hole in the forecastle floor and found the water nearly up to it. We were satisfied she could not be kept afloat, and lowered the boat," Captain Kerr said. The sailors put Kerr's wife, Martha in the lifeboat and took her to the schooner *A. J. Dewey*, the third vessel in the string, which was standing nearby. The seas were still high and it was an exhausting experience for Mrs. Kerr, but she made it safely. Once he knew she was safe, Kerr returned to his sinking command to get his books and papers from the cabin. By then he said "we found water even with the top of the hatches forward. In less than ten minutes after we left her, and an hour after the collision, she went down head foremost in thirty or forty fathoms of water." He said air pressure caused the ship to explode as it sank. Pieces of the main deck and cabins floated back to the surface.

Capt. Kerr seemed partial to square rigged ships. He returned to the lakes in 1884 after he bought the bark *Constitution.* At age sixty-two, he planned to retire. He was making what was to have been his final trip on the *Constitution* when he was accidentally knocked overboard by a swinging boom and drowned. It happened on the Detroit River on October 30, 1887. His son, Robert W. Kerr, was serving as mate aboard the *Sunny Side* when it was lost, and also was on the *Constitution*, when the captain was killed.

The *Sunny Side* originally was rigged as a schooner when launched at Detroit in 1862. The ship measured one hundred sixty-four feet in length and had three masts.

Sources:

      Beers, J. H. & Co., Chicago, "Captain Robert Kerr," from History of the Great Lakes Illustrated, Volume II, page 854.

      Cleveland Herald, "The Sinking of the *Sunnyside*," and "How the *Sunnyside* Went Down," Aug. 23 and 24, respectively, 1883, news clips, Institute for Great Lakes Research, Perrysburg, O.

      Detroit Free Press, "The *Sunnyside* Sunk," Aug. 22, 1883, microfilm rolls, State Library of Michigan, Lansing, Mich.

Collision in a Lake Erie Gale

The scene is chaos. It is sometime after midnight the morning of Friday, April 29, 1887. The place is a black and deadly spot on storm whipped Lake Erie, perhaps a few miles off Port Stanley, Ontario. Through the screaming of the wind and maddening rumble of the sea can be heard the steady throbbing of a working steam engine, a man-made machine operated by men who dare to use it to do battle against the unleashed power of nature. Slowly out of the dark emerges the faint lantern lights of the tug *Martin Swain* with five cargo-laden schooners in tow. Sailors stand on the decks of all six ships, each secretly questioning his or her own sanity for daring to venture out in such a gale. Even with its engine operating at full power, with the engineer delivering all of the steam his machinery is capable of making, the tug and its line of consorts is at a stand-still and the storm is intensifying.

At some point, the captain of the *Swain,* a man whose identity appears lost in the dust-covered records of this moment in history, decided that he had had enough. He gave the order to turn the tug around and make a run for shelter, perhaps to the lee of Long Point. Slowly, as the *Swain* made its turn, the steamer's line of consorts, the *H. W. Sage, Thomas W. Parker, Louie O'Neil, Riverside* and *D. S. Austin,* began following in faithful order. The masters of each of the schooners, aware of the *Swain's* turn away from the teeth of the storm, were all on their decks, shouting orders to the crews and being annoyed at the way the storm carried away their voices of authority. The wind now would be at their sterns. They had mixed feelings about the course change. Each vessel could raise sail and help the tug race to a point of safety, but with the seas pounding from behind, the skippers understood that they were in for a rough ride. There was much confusion. It was at this moment that the main tow line leading from the tug parted. All five schooners dropped off into the gloom where the *Parker* and *O'Neil* collided.

Captain Amza L. Fitch, master of the *Parker,* said he had his ship in stays but the *O'Neil* had canvas raised at the moment the tow line broke. The *O'Neil,* which was directly behind the *Parker,* couldn't stop its momentum and the two vessels hit, their masts, ropes and canvas getting tangled. Fitch said the *Parker's* jibboom went into the *O'Neil's* foresail, breaking off the latter's main and mizzen masts. After the *O'Neil's* spars toppled, the two ships drifted away from one another. Fitch said that before they were out of shouting range, he asked Thomas Walker, master of the *O'Neil,* if his ship was taking on water. He said Walker answered "no."

If Walker said that, either he hadn't had time to assess his situation or he misunderstood the question. The coal-laden *O'Neil* was sinking under his feet even as he spoke. The collision had punctured the schooner's side and the vessel was sunk almost to the decks by the time the crew had the life boat launched and the last man, Captain Walker, was safely away. As they pulled off into the storm-tossed seas, the eight sailors said they quickly lost sight of their doomed vessel. All they saw was a lone lantern, still burning from the stern where they had pulled away from the ship. The lamp disappeared about three minutes later. There was an ominous rumble from deep below as air pressure from the sinking vessel blew away the hatches and cabin. The *O'Neil* was gone.

Walker said the wind was blowing from the northeast and the seas were as high as he could ever recall in his years of sailing the lakes. All the sailors could do at first was put the bow of their frail craft into the seas and hold it there, letting the boat drift before the wind toward the eastern end of Lake Erie and Buffalo. Dawn came and then the day passed without sight of land or a passing ship. At sundown, the wind shifted to the west, but the seas did not diminish. The sailors were cold and wet, and some of the men were suffering from exposure and frost bite. Walker worried that another day in the boat would claim lives. That night, at abut 9:00 PM, when the Conneaut Light was sighted, the captain decided to take a chance. He ordered his men to pull broadside against the seas and make for a landing at Conneaut. He knew he was taking a chance of getting the boat overturned and possibly drowning everybody, but time was running out. It worked. The boat was successfully brought to shore. The sailors landed not far from Conneaut where a farmer gave them shelter.

One crew member, Sherman Williams, of Marine City, Michigan, was hospitalized for treatment of frost bite and general exposure. He recovered. The other survivors included William Peel, George Thomas and Margaret Barrett, all of Marine City, Daniel Nathan of Cartwright, Ontario, and Charles Kenny of Oscoda, Michigan.

Sources:
    Chicago Inter Ocean, "Safety of the *O'Neil's* Crew," May 3, 1887, news clipping, Institute for Great Lakes Research, Perrysburg, O.
    Detroit Free Press, "Sunk Off Port Stanley," May 2, and "A Crew's Perils," May 3, 1887, news clippings, Institute for Great Lakes Research, Perrysburg, O.
    Detroit Morning Tribune, "Barge *Louis O'Neil* Sunk," May 2, 1887, microfilm rolls, State Library of Michigan, Lansing, Mich.
    Marquette Mining Journal, Marquette, Mich., "The Wrecked *O'Neil*," news clipping, Institute for Great Lakes Research, Perrysburg, O.

*The **Northern Queen** was known in its day as a "ship killer." It collided with and sank three other vessels between 1891 and 1912. Courtesy Institute for Great Lakes Research.*

Clash with a Ship Killer

The Northern Transportation Company's steel freighter *Northern Queen* was known in its day as a ship killer. People in the Thumb District of Michigan remember the *Queen* as the ship that sank the *North Star* when the two vessels collided in fog off Port Sanilac in 1908. At least two other wrecks lie on the bottom of the Great Lakes following entanglements with the *Northern Queen*. The steamer *G. J. Grammer* was sunk in a fog shrouded crash with the *Queen* off Corsich Shoals in 1912, and the wooden schooner *Fayette Brown* was run down and sunk on Lake Erie on June 4, 1891.

The *Brown* was the *Queen's* first and perhaps its most defenseless victim. The three-masted schooner was heavily laden with iron ore, on the last leg of a trip from Marquette to Fairport, Ohio, when the accident happened a few miles from the mouth of the Detroit River. The crew of the *Brown* said the schooner was beating its way out in the lake in "thick weather" at about 2:00 AM when the lights of an approaching steamer were seen off the port bow. Moments later, the two vessels hit almost bow on. The *Brown* measured one hundred and seventy-eight feet in length while the steel hulled *Queen* was three hundred and twelve feet long. It was no contest. The coal laden *Queen* demolished the little schooner and sent it directly to the bottom.

As often happens in ship collisions, one sailor climbed aboard the *Northern Queen* before the two hulls separated. The rest of the *Brown's* crew scrambled into the overhead rigging as the schooner dropped under their feet in about sixty feet of water. Fortunately, the wreck remained upright and the sailors saved themselves by hanging on the masts and crosstrees until help arrived. They were rescued by the steamer *Robert Mills* about an hour later.

In the meantime, the master of the *Northern Queen* continued his trip to Duluth. They said he stopped briefly at Detroit to file a protest against the owners of the *Brown,* apparently angry because their vessel got in his way. The newspapers of the day failed to reveal the name of the *Queen's* skipper. The *Duluth Daily News* suggested in a story on June 5 that what he did was "apparent cowardly action."

Sources:

   Detroit Free Press, "Collision on Lake Erie," Jun. 5, 1891, microfilm rolls, State Library of Michigan, Lansing, Mich.

   Duluth Daily News, "Sunk in Collision," and "Preparation for a Suit," June 5 and June 8, respectively, news clips, Institute for Great Lakes Research, Perrysburg, O.

   Greenwood, John O., "Steamer *Northern Queen (2),*" Namesakes 1910-1919, Freshwater Press, Inc., Cleveland, O., 1986.

   Stayer, Pat and Jim, *"North Star, "* Shipwrecks of Sanilac, Lakeshore Press, 1989.

Fire

In the days of wooden sailing ships, a fire at sea was a most dreaded event. Probably because of the extreme caution taken by sailors, it was uncommon to hear a report of a schooner fire on the Great Lakes.

*The schooner **St. Lawrence** was one of the few sailing ships destroyed by fire on the lakes. It burned on Lake Michigan in 1878. Courtesy Institute for Great Lakes Research.*

Burning of the *St. Lawrence*

The schooner *St. Lawrence* was one of those that burned. This ship was lost on Lake Michigan, about twenty miles from Milwaukee, Wisconsin, on April 30, 1878. The *St. Lawrence*, under the command of Capt. Martin Larkins, was a leaky thirty-six-year-old boat, considered among the oldest sailing vessels on the lakes. It should not be surprising that the fire started about 2:00 PM from a kettle of pitch, which boiled over on a galley stove. Pitch, or coal tar, was commonly used to plug leaky joints on wooden ships. While it was a good sealant against moisture, tar also is flammable. By the time the fire was discovered, it was too late to save the *St. Lawrence*.

As the sailors battled the fire and tried to keep it from spreading, Captain Larkins and a passenger, Arthur Piplow, worked to launch the ship's only lifeboat. It was a dangerous thing to be doing because the schooner's sails were set and the *St. Lawrence* was still underway, moving at an estimated speed of about six miles an hour. The moment the boat dropped from the davits into the water, it capsized. Both men tumbled overboard where they drowned. The four sailors still riding the burning schooner were shaken by the tragedy. They were temporarily undecided as to what to do. Some wanted to bring the ship around and attempt a rescue. Common sense, however, dictated the necessary course of action. Their own lives were in great danger. Also they knew it would be impossible to manage the sails on the burning vessel to make a turn. This fact, and the fire's advance, made the decision for them.

The men were busy stripping wooden planks from the ship and building a makeshift raft when the schooner *Granada* saw the fire and drew alongside for a dramatic rescue. It only took a moment for the crew to leap to the *Granada's* deck, but in that brief time, the fire might easily have claimed both vessels. The *Granada* escaped the fire fiend that day. The *St. Lawrence* was laden with lumber and bound for a Wisconsin port when it burned and sank somewhere off Milwaukee.

Sources:
Chicago Inter Ocean, "Burning of the Schooner *St. Lawrence,*" and "The *St. Lawrence,*" May 2 and May 3, 1878, newspaper clippings, Institute for Great Lakes Research, Perrysburg, O.
Master data sheets, Institute for Great Lakes Research, Perrysburg, O.

The **F. B. Gardner** *was rigged as a schooner-barge when it burned and sank in Lake Huron. Courtesy Institute for Great Lakes Research.*

The Ship of Many Faces

From the time it slid down the ways at Sheboygan, Wisconsin in 1855, until claimed by fire on Lake Huron in 1904, the *F. B. Gardner* was a ship of many faces. First rigged as a brig, or two-masted square-rigged sailing vessel, the *Gardner* was transformed eleven years later to be a barque. A third mast was installed and the ship's bowsprit was shortened, giving the vessel an entirely different appearance. Then in 1872, the owners changed the *Gardner* again, this time making a schooner out of it. Two years after that, the vessel was stripped of its upper masts and converted to be a barge in tow behind a steamer.

The *Gardner* was still faithfully serving as a barge when it became one of the rare lake sailing ships to be destroyed by fire. It happened at about 5:00 AM on September 15, when the *Gardner* was in tow behind the steam barge *D. Leuty,* for an upbound trip. The cause of the blaze was never explained. Once the fire was discovered, the *Leuty* pulled alongside the burning craft and crews from both ships battled the flames. When the fire reached the *Gardner's* cargo of coal the sailors found there was no hope of saving the ship. The *Gardner* was abandoned and left to burn until it sank.

The *Gardner* went down in about fifty feet of water, about six miles northeast of Port Sanilac, Michigan. It later was torn apart with dynamite because the schooner sank in relatively shallow water and was considered a hazard to other ships. Divers still visit the remains of the wreck which lie inside the Sanilac Shores Underwater Preserve.

Sources:

     Port Huron Daily Times, Sept. 16, 1904, microfilm roll, St. Clair County Library, Port Huron, Mich.

     Raymond, Oliver, notes on events of 1904, from his book Shingle Shavers and Berry Pickers, self-published.

     Stayer, Pat and Jim, *"F. B. Gardner,"* Shipwrecks of Sanilac, Lakeshore Press, 1989.

Jinxed Ship *Crosthwaite*

Sailors have traditionally been a superstitious lot. When the schooner *William Crosthwaite* burned while anchored off Lake Superior's Whitefish Point on November 13, 1904, Capt. Frank Patterson said he wasn't surprised. "I would think I was hoodooed," he remarked. He said the crew escaped the fire in a lifeboat from the steamer *Sitka,* wrecked one month earlier on Au Sable Reef, off Grand Marais, Michigan, and the boat's oars came from the steamer *Waverly,* sunk in a collision on Lake Huron one year earlier. Not only this, but Patterson said one member of his crew was a survivor when the schooner *F. B. Gardner* burned in September near Port Sanilac, Michigan, also in Lake Huron (see above story). With all of these combined remnants of bad luck gathered on the decks of the *Crosthwaite* at the same time, Patterson reasoned that it was logical to expect the worst.

The fire came in the midst of trouble. The *Crosthwaite* was traveling up the lake empty, in tow behind the steam barge *E. N. Saunders,* when the two ships anchored behind Whitefish Point to escape the brunt of a northwesterly gale. They were in company with a big fleet of vessels, all waiting out the storm before venturing out into the open waters of the lake. The crew of the *Crosthwaite* used the time to heat water from a stove in the forecastle to do their laundry. The stove was left unguarded at about 6:00 PM while the crew went to the galley to eat their supper. The meal was interrupted when fire broke out in the forecastle. By the time the blaze was known, it was already out of control. Years of oiling the wooden decks and sealing the ship's cracks with tar created a rich source of fuel for a fire that no man could stop. Captain Patterson said his first thought was to try to reach his cabin near the bow to rescue some personal papers and his wallet, containing about two hundred dollars. The fire was so hot he was driven back to the stern.

Luckily the ship's lifeboat was mounted on davits at the stern. The fire spread so fast across the oily decks the crew barely had time to launch the boat and get away. They escaped into the winter storm, wearing only the clothes they took with them to the supper table. By the time they reached the *Saunders,* the men were suffering from exposure. Everybody came out of it alive.

The *Crosthwaite* was raised the next year to sail again. The record shows that the schooner remained on the Great Lakes registry until it was sunk in a collision with the steamer *Homer Warren* on Lake Erie in September, 1906. That means the hull was raised and rebuilt in 1905. The old barge saw one more year of service after the fire. The ship was on the lakes a total of forty years. It was named for William Crosthwaite, the man who built it at Bay City, Michigan, in 1866.

Sources:

Detroit Free Press, "*Crosthwaite* Burned at Her Anchorage," Nov. 15, 1904, news clipping, Institute for Great Lakes Research, Perrysburg, O.

Greenwood, John O., "Schooner-Barge *William Crosthwaite,*" Namesakes 1900-1919, Freshwater Press, Inc., Cleveland, O., 1987, p. 452.

Marquette Daily Mining Journal, "Loss of the *Crosthwaite,*" Nov. 16, 1904, news clipping, Institute for Great Lakes Research, Perrysburg, O.

Master data file, Institute for Great Lakes Research, Perrysburg, O.

Spontaneous Combustion

The fire that destroyed the schooner *Ogarita* was blamed on spontaneous combustion, although nobody ever tried to explain how that could happen in a hold filled with cold, damp chunks of coal.

The fire broke out in the hold at about 10:30 PM on October 25, 1905, while the schooner was in tow behind the steam barge *Zillah* off Thunder Bay in northern Lake Huron. As the crews from both ships fought the flames, the lights from the fire were spotted by the life saving service at Alpena, and a boat was sent out to assist. The burning cargo of coal on a wooden ship in the middle of Lake Huron proved to be an impossible obstacle. After hours of doing battle, the sailors finally gave up and left the doomed *Ogarita* to float away and burn itself to oblivion.

The Alpena-based tug *Ralph* steamed out later that morning in a belated attempt to extinguish the fire and tow the vessel into port where something, perhaps the hull and a portion of the cargo, might be saved. The crew of the tug said the schooner was a mass of flame and they could not get close enough to do anything. The *Ogarita* burned until it sank. Nobody knows just where or when it happened.

Ironically, the vessel's Indian name came from the Sioux language. It means "to scatter to the winds."

Sources:

Detroit Free Press, "*Ogarita* Still Burning," Oct. 27, 1905, news clippings, Institute for Great Lakes Research, Perrysburg, O.

Duluth Evening Herald, "Schooner In Flames," Oct. 26, 1905, news clippings, Institute for Great Lakes Research, Perrysburg, O.

Greenwood, John O., "Schooner *Ogarita*," Namesakes 1900-1909, Freshwater Press, Cleveland, O., 1987, page 28.

*Schooner-barge **Dorcas Pendell** burned at Harbor Beach, Michigan in 1914. Courtesy Institute for Great Lakes Research.*

The Fourteenth Casualty

The official count of ships lost in the Great Storm of 1913 was thirteen. In truth, there was a fourteenth ship lost, even though it was indirectly related to the storm, and the final destruction didn't happen for another two months. It was the schooner-barge *Dorcas Pendell,* a thirty-year-old worn-out vessel that had seen better days but was still plying the lakes.

The *Pendell* was moored inside the breakwaters at Harbor Beach, Michigan, when the storm struck Lake Huron on November 9. At first nobody worried about the barge because it was inside the protective walls of the town's mile-wide artificial harbor. The storm of 1913 was no ordinary blow, however. The wind, measured at hurricane strength, whipped the harbor with such fury that the schooner broke loose and drifted ashore. The powerful seas and high tides created by the gale carried the old ship so far inland that when the storm was over, the hull was resting upright, in only four feet of water. The *Pendell*'s hull was so deeply embedded in the mud that tugs couldn't pull it free. Plans were made to dig a channel to free the ship the following spring.

In the meantime, a watchman was hired to stay aboard the vessel for the winter to protect it from vandals. All went well until the night of January 5, 1914. It was an especially cold day and the watchman put extra coal in the stove to warm his quarters. The stove overheated, the *Dorcas Pendell* took fire and was destroyed. Fragments of the hull still lie in the mud.

Sources:
Harbor Beach Times, Jan. 9, 1914, from bound newspaper volumes stored at city clerk's office, Harbor Beach, Mich.
Master data sheets, Institute for Great Lakes Research, Perrysburg, O.

River Crashes

All ships hauling between Buffalo and Chicago, or from Duluth and out through the St. Lawrence Seaway, must pass through the St. Clair River. Some of the accidents, especially during the days when sailing ships were among the travelers, were spectacular.

Complex River Crack-up

As long as ships have been carrying passengers and freight on the Great Lakes, they have converged on the St. Clair River. That river, linking Lakes Huron and Erie and separating the two port cities of Port Huron, Michigan, and Sarnia, Ontario, remains among the busiest water courses in the world. Back when there were more ships traversing the lakes, massive traffic jams were common. Port Huron's Black River, which empties into the St. Clair River, served as a crossroads for vessels ferrying people, railroad cars and supplies between the two communities. All ships hauling between Buffalo and Chicago, or from Duluth and out through the St. Lawrence Seaway, must pass through the St. Clair River. Some of the accidents, especially during the days when sailing ships were among the travelers there, were spectacular.

The collisions and sinkings on the night of April 29, 1880 may have set a record for the number of vessels damaged in one ongoing chain of events. The night's happenings developed into something of a comedy of errors, although nobody was laughing. Miraculously there were no injuries.

The trouble started when the captain of the schooner *Walter H. Oades* dropped anchor in the middle of the river. Ships were still being lighted with oil and kerosene lanterns and their lights were not easily seen at night, especially if there was a little smoke or fog in the air. That might explain why the steamship *Chicago* collided with the *Oades*. The steamer's bow struck the schooner in the port cathead, near the stern, cutting the smaller vessel open below the water line. The impact cut the *Oades'* anchor cable and the schooner drifted off, capsized and sank on its side along the river bank about a mile below Sarnia. The *Chicago* went out of control and ran aground with its stern partially blocking the river.

A few minutes later the schooner *Charles Foster* came on the scene. The *Foster* had its sails set and was beating its way upriver against the current. The wheelsman could not bring the ship clear of the steamer and there was another collision. The crash caused extensive damage to the *Foster's* sails and rigging. After drifting away from the *Chicago*, the *Foster's* master dropped anchor in mid-stream. He planned to wait until morning to assess the damage.

Next came the downbound tug *Castle* with three lumber barges, *Fannie Neil, John A. McDougall* and *Anglo-Saxon* in tow. The tug's crew spotted the *Chicago* and brought its consorts safely around that obstacle, but the vessels then tangled with the *Foster*. The tug captain chose to dodge to the Canadian side of the river to pass the schooner and the wheelsman on the *Neil* followed. The helmsman of the *McDougall* missed seeing the danger, steered for the American side of the river and the barge collided head-on with the *Foster*, carrying away its bobstays and more of its sails and rigging. The crash tossed sleeping sailors out of their bunks in the *McDougall's* forecastle. The bow of the *McDougall* was badly crushed and it was leaking. The ship was taken to Detroit for repair. It took workers more than a week to get the *Oades* raised and in dry dock for repair. The *Chicago* was pulled off the river bank the next morning.

Sources:
    Detroit Free Press, "A Chapter of Accidents at Port Huron," May 1, 1880, microfilm files, State Library of Michigan, Lansing, Mich.
    Port Huron Daily Times, "Marine News," Apr. 30, 1880, microfilm files, State Library of Michigan, Lansing, Mich.

A Mid-River Crash

A collision of two sailing ships was always messy. Not only was the striking of the hulls a bone-jarring experience, but then sails, masts and rigging always got tangled and broken. Anybody standing on the open deck was in danger of being seriously hurt or killed by a rain of falling spars, ropes and pulleys.

This was what happened when the downbound and grain-laden barkentine *J. G. Masten* collided with the schooner *Maid of the Mist* in the early morning of September 10, 1871, just below the Port Huron town limits. The *Masten's* skipper, Capt. James Kendrick was blamed for the accident because his ship hit the *Maid of the Mist* while it was anchored for the night on the river. A judge ruled that the barkentine was traveling too fast.

Kendrick said he was standing forward on the *Masten's* deck when the faint image of the schooner was spotted about one hundred feet ahead at about 2:00 AM. He said he ordered the wheelsman to turn hard to starboard, but it was too late. The bow of the *Masten* struck the schooner on the starboard side, carrying away its jib boom, head gear and foremast head, breaking the starboard stanchions and driving the *Masten's* anchor through the side of the hull. The schooner sank about ninety minutes later. By then Capt. John Jones and the four members of his crew had abandoned ship. Nobody was hurt.

Captain Kendrick said the *Masten* was traveling about six miles an hour after entering the headwaters of the river from Lake Huron, and his crew was taking in sail when the accident happened. He said he was standing forward near the lookout when the anchored schooner was spotted dead ahead. Both Kendrick and the lookout, George Johnson, testified that they saw no lights on the *Maid of the Mist.*

A court of inquiry at Detroit awarded damages to the owners of the *Maid of the Mist.* Not only was the bark traveling recklessly, but the court said its crew failed to see the lights of the anchored schooner before it was too late. The court believed Jones when he said the lamps were lit and hanging in their proper place.

Sources:

Detroit Daily Post, record of the court proceedings, June 5, 1872, microfilm rolls, State Library of Michigan, Lansing, Mi.

Port Huron Weekly Times, Sept. 14, 1871, microfilm rolls, St. Clair Public Library, Port Huron, Mi.

The *Tremble* and *Ben Hur*

The broken remains of the schooners *Ben Hur* and *M. E. Tremble* lie together on the river bottom at Port Huron. The wrecks, each consisting of a hull partly filled with mud, can be found in the narrow rapids, just south of the Blue Water Bridge. The *Tremble* sank after a collision with the steamer *W. E. Wetmore* on September 8, 1890. The *Ben Hur* accident was directly related to the *Tremble* sinking. This vessel was sunk in a second collision while involved in an attempted salvage operation at the *Tremble* two months later.

The wrecking began when the upbound *Tremble,* under the command of Capt. Charles Pitcher, was hit in the starboard quarter by the downbound steamer *Wetmore* at about 1:30 AM on September 8. The *Tremble* was filled with coal and under tow behind the steamer *B. W. Blanchard.* The two vessels met the *Wetmore* and its tow, the barge *Brunette,* at the rapids where the river bends. The *Blanchard* whistled to show that it intended to pass on the Canadian side of the river. The *Wetmore* returned the proper signal to indicate that the helmsman understood. The *Blanchard* turned to starboard to make room for the approaching vessel and the two steamers passed within about two hundred feet of each other. The wheelsman on the *Tremble,* however, didn't compensate for the change in course quickly enough and the two ships hit. The schooner sank in three minutes. Most of the crew was caught asleep so there was a mad scramble. In their haste to get away in the only life boat, one sailor, identified in news stories as either William McFall or William McMaugh, was left behind. His cries were heard and the sailors tried to go back for him but it was too late. The *Tremble* sank and the forgotten crew member was seen no more. A fifty dollar reward was offered for his body.

In the meantime, the Grand Trunk railroad car ferry *Huron* was crossing the river from Port Huron with eight sleeping cars filled with passengers. The *Huron* saw the accident and stopped to pick up survivors. While standing by in midstream, the ferry was rammed by the passing steamer *Rufus P. Ranney.* The crash rocked the car ferry so violently

A dynamite blast clears away the upper works of the ill-fated schooner **M. E. Tremble** *after the vessel sank in the St. Clair River at Port Huron. Courtesy Institute for Great Lakes Research.*

there was concern that the railroad cars would break free and roll off into the river. The crash awoke passengers who were sleeping in the Pullman train cars and there were a few minutes of panic. The railroad cars remained in their place. Neither the *Ranney* nor the *Huron* sank, but both vessels were severely damaged.

A Port Huron businessman, Henry McMorran, tried to salvage the *Tremble*. He purchased the schooner *Ben Hur,* and formed the Murphy Salvage Company. On November 8, exactly two months after the *Tremble* was sunk, a similar accident sent the *Ben Hur* to the bottom. The steamer *Passaic* and a string of barges passed the anchored schooner in the dark of night. One of the barges, the *Superior,* got too close and collided with the *Ben Hur*. Again, nobody was hurt.

Now there were two schooners on the bottom and both of them were a threat to river navigation. Further attempts at salvage were abandoned. Dynamite was used to destroy the upper works of both the *Ben Hur* and the *Tremble*. The blast removed the cabins, decks and spars, but the hulls are still resting where they sank.

Sources:
    Duluth Weekly Herald, Duluth, Minn., "The Wreck of the *Tremble*," Sept. 12, 1890, news clipping, Institute for Great Lakes Research, Perrysburg, O.
    Kohl, Cris, "Shipwreck Tales: The St. Clair River (to 1900)," pp 131-134, self published, 1987.
    Marquette Daily Mining Journal, Marquette, Mich., "Sinking of Barge *Tremble,* Sept. 9, 1890, news clipping, Institute for Great Lakes Research, Perrysburg, O.

*Schooner **Fontana** lies half sunk in the St. Clair River after a collision with the **Santiago** in 1900. From Cris Kohl collection.*

The Great River Menace

The schooner *Fontana* is best remembered for the trouble it caused after it sank from a collision at the head of the St. Clair River at Port Huron. In the end, the wreck was blasted into kindling after it sank one other vessel, was linked to two accidental deaths, and caused extensive damage to at least two other ships. The *Fontana* was laden with iron ore, in tow behind the steamer *Kaliyuga,* when it collided with the upbound barge *Santiago* on the night of August 3, 1900. The crash stove in the bow of the ill-fated schooner and it sank bow first within minutes. Crew member John McGregor, of Erie, Pennsylvania, who was asleep in the forecastle, was killed in the accident. The others, Capt. George McCoy, mate Ed Vissey, Neil McLeod, John Liegmund, N. Mulvaney and Ben McLeod escaped in the life boat.

The *Santiago,* which was upbound in tow behind the steamer *Appomattox,* was not seriously damaged. Its master, Capt. Frank Hebner, refused to comment about the accident. The *Port Huron Daily Times* speculated that one, or perhaps both barges drifted too close to the center of the river and failed to see each other's lights because of fog.

At first the owners of the *Fontana,* the Cleveland Cliffs Iron Co., Cleveland, had high hopes of raising the schooner. The two hundred and thirty-one-foot-long vessel came to a rest with its bow submerged in about fifty feet of water and its stern resting on a river bank, in only twenty feet of water. The *Fontana's* masts, stern and after cabin were still above water. Because it was in a narrow and well traveled channel of the river, precautions were made to protect the wreck from further accidents. Two buoys were placed in the river to mark the wreck, and two lights were placed on the exposed portion of the hull. Before salvagers had a chance to start working on the *Fontana,* however, the accidents began. The very next day the schooner *Kingfisher,* a consort behind the steamer *Samuel Marshall,* hit the wreck straight on. The accident carried away the *Fontana's* foretop and main masts, and caused extensive additional damage to the hull. For a few hours the *Kingfisher* was wedged on top of the submerged wreck. After the local tug *Brockway* pulled it free, it was found that the *Kingfisher* suffered extensive hull damage.

The *Daily Times* said on August 5 that "since the collision there have been several narrow escapes of vessels. Robert McCullough, who is watching on the wreck for the Kendall Marine Reporting Company, noticed a boat coming into the course which would evidently run into the wreck. He blew a fog horn danger signal and yelled to the skipper to port his wheel. The wheel was ported and the steamer narrowly escaped the wreck. The skipper expressed his thanks for the timely warning." After a few weeks of mishaps, the decision was made. The *Fontana* was to be destroyed by dynamite. Salvagers agreed that the current was too swift and the river too busy to risk trying to raise the ship. The Harris Baker Company of Detroit was hired to do the work. Before workers arrived on the scene, however, the schooner *John Martin,* in tow behind the steamer *Maurice B. Grover,* was sunk a few hundred feet away in a collision with the upbound steamer *Yuma* on September 2 (See *Martin* story below). Now two wrecks were creating a hazard to navigation in the same area. The tug *F. J. Hayes* was stationed like a lightship at the mouth of the river as an extra warning to passing ships.

A few days later a sailor from the schooner *A. J. McBrier,* was knocked overboard and drowned when his ship got caught in the rapids and tried to veer out of the way of one of the wrecks. In the excitement the *McBrier* ground to a stop on top of the *Fontana.* It had to be pulled free by tugs and then taken to dry dock for repair.

Dynamite was used to destroy both the *Fontana* and *Martin.* The hulls of both wrecks still lie on the bottom of the river.

Sources:
    Port Huron Daily Times, "Collision in the Rapids," Aug. 4, and "Menace to Navigation," Aug. 5, 1900, microfilm rolls, State Library of Michigan, Lansing, Mich.
    Van Der Linden, Rev. Peter, Marine Historical Society of Detroit, *"Fontana,"* from Great Lakes Ships We Remember II, p. 117.

Sinking of The *John Martin*

Wheelsman George Kyle was one of four survivors of the wreck of the schooner *John Martin* because he left his post and scrambled up the mizzen mast while the ship sank under his feet. Four other shipmates were not as lucky. They either died in the crash, drowned or were trapped below deck.

The *Martin,* a two hundred and twenty-foot-long vessel, was laden with ore the night it collided with the steel steamer *Yuma* on the St. Clair River. The hull opened up and the wooden schooner sank so quickly there was no time to escape. The accident happened at about 8:00 PM on September 21, 1900, on the Michigan side of the river about one hun-

*The **John Martin** sank at Port Huron after a collision in 1900. Four sailors died. Courtesy Institute for Great Lakes Research.*

dred yards north of where the Blue Water Bridge stands today. The wreck still rests in the same spot, in about sixty feet of water and right beside the schooner *Fontana*. Sport divers visit, but the site is considered dangerous because of strong river currents.

Kyle and seaman Gabriel Peterson were both at the helm as the schooner, under tow behind the steamer *Maurice H. Grover,* commanded by Capt. Ed Mooney, entered the river from Lake Huron. At the same time the coal laden steamer *Yuma,* Capt. Daniel Bule, was approaching from the south. The *Yuma* was off its course and traveling closer to the American side of the river than it should have been. The two steamers nearly sideswiped when they passed within fifty feet of each other. The crew of the *Martin* didn't realize the danger until it was too late. Kyle said he first knew the ship was in trouble when Capt. James Lawless shouted from the quarter deck to turn the wheel hard to starboard. As he was spinning the wheel, he looked up and saw the lights of the steamer bearing down on the schooner from only a few feet away. It was too late for the *Martin* to get out of the way.

The *Yuma* struck the doomed schooner in the starboard bow. "She walked right through us to the mizzen," said Kyle. "I ran up the mizzen rigging on the port side, Peterson following." He said the *Martin* sank so fast that it dropped under the hull of the *Yuma* before the steamer could back away. Kyle and Peterson both climbed for their lives, but before they could get out of danger, they were drawn under water with the sinking ship. When they surfaced, they grabbed wreckage, probably one of the masts, and held on until they were rescued. The *Martin* sank in an upright position and the masts were visible above the water. The two sailors were picked up by Port Huron marine reporter R. A. Christier, who heard the crash and took his personal boat out to the scene. Christier said the noise of the collision was heard for about a mile away.

Two other survivors, Walter Wendel and Rudolph See, both of Cleveland, were asleep in the forecastle. The crash threw them from their bunks. They made their way out of the sunken wreck and swam to the surface, where they were picked up by a lifeboat from the *Yuma*. Captain Lawless perished in the accident, as did mate William Ross, the ship's steward, identified only as Mrs. Bacon of Cleveland, and a fourth, unidentified sailor.

As explained earlier, both the *Martin* and *Fontana* created a problem for navigation because they were sunk in the rapids, in one of the narrowest spots on the St. Clair River. When efforts to remove the ships failed, dynamite was used to remove the masts and clear the way for passing ships.

Source:
  Detroit Free Press, "Schooner *Martin* Sunk," Sept. 22, 1900, microfilm files, State Library of Michigan, Lansing.

Sliding to the Bottom

Few ships have been sunk as fast as the schooner-barge *Fostoria* after it collided with a large block of floating ice. It happened at 8:00 PM on May 10, 1901, as the coal laden barge and one other schooner, the *E. C. Roberts,* were being pulled through the rapids near the head of the St. Clair River by the steamer *Annie Laura* and assisting tug *Agyle.* It had been a particularly hard winter and large chunks of ice were still tumbling their way through the river following the spring break-up of ice on lower Lake Huron.

Capt. James A. Lockhart, master of the *Fostoria,* told a reporter for the *Port Huron Daily Times* how it happened. "It was quite foggy on the river and the current was running swift. My son. D. O. Lockhart, who is captain of the steamer which tows us, thought it best to get the assistance of a tug to help him out of the rapids and whistled for one. The tug *Argyle* came alongside and took a line from the steamer. We had gotten up as far as the light house and were going along nicely, the river being almost clear of boats, when without a moment's warning we heard a crash and the mate yelled 'she's going down.' The *Fostoria* seemed to have been struck on the port bow, as she listed over to that side before going under."

Burt Sharpe, who was fishing on the river, said the *Fostoria* seemed to dive bow first after it hit the ice. "I heard the boat's crew ringing bells and blowing horns, but the steam barge which was working hard to get out into the lake, paid no attention to the calls. First the bow of the *Fostoria* went under water. I could see the lights disappear. I watched the light on the top of one of the spars and soon that disappeared beneath the water. There was no out cry and I came to the conclusion that the entire crew was drowned. I don't believe it was over two minutes from the time the boat struck the cake of ice before she was under water."

Captain Lockhart described the confusion aboard the sinking ship: "The men all ran aft and began to clear away the yawl. We succeeded in getting the boat partly lowered, but the painter became jammed and we had no time to look for an ax. The boat was going down with us and taking us under with the suction. I grabbed my daughter just as we went down and soon come to the top with my arms still around her. A box floated by. I think it was the cover off the steering gear. We caught hold of it. I could see two or three of the crew around me and thought they were all right. We drifted for a while, but found it hard work to hang on as the water was so cold. The tug came along, threw us a line and pulled us aboard." Lockhart and his daughter, Annie Lockhard, the ship's cook, were saved, as was sailor Elmer Conk, who was found clinging to a piece of ice. Two other crew members, mate William Schlitt and sailor Walter Strobel, were apparently overcome by the cold and drowned before the *Argyle* found them.

The *Argyle's* skipper, Capt. J. S. Moore, said he noticed that the *Fostoria* was sinking but couldn't break away from the tow and get back to be of any assistance before the schooner was gone. He said the water was so cold that the three people that were rescued would probably have been dead in another few minutes. The survivors were taken ashore where they received medical attention.

Sources:
    Greenwood, John O., "Schooner *Fostoria,*" Namesakes 1900-1909, Freshwater Press, Inc., Cleveland, Ohio, 1987, p 407
    Port Huron Daily Times, "Two Lives Lost," May 11, 1901, microfilm rolls, State Library of Michigan, Lansing, Mich.

Bad Omen

To many people the number thirteen is a most unlucky number. Capt. William Bonnah of Toledo worried because his newly purchased vessel, the schooner *John Schuette,* was his thirteenth ship. That he agreed to buy the ship on March 13, 1909, was too much of a coincidence. When he noticed the date on a wall calendar, he insisted on waiting until the next day to close the deal. Bonnah's superstitions seemed to have been well founded. Four months later the *Schuette* was wrecked in a collision with the steamer *Alfred Mitchell* on the Detroit River.

*If the schooner **John Schuette** had any luck at all, it was bound to be bad. Courtesy Institute for Great Lakes Research.*

The captain counted it as bad luck that his schooner was lost. Thousands of other people, who were nearly caught up in the accident when the *Schuette* narrowly missed hitting a crowded excursion liner, probably agreed with him. The good news was that nobody was hurt. The crew, including the captain's wife and sister who were along for the trip, also escaped.

The *Schuette* was carrying coal, bound from Cleveland to Lake Superior, when the accident happened near Ecorse at about 7:00 PM on July 2. The thirty-four-year-old schooner was under sail and beating its way up river, against the cur-

81

rent, when a summer squall blew the vessel off its course. As the crew struggled to get their wayward ship under control, the *Schuette* drifted into the path of the down bound excursion steamer *Columbia*. The *Columbia,* under the command of Capt. John Wilkinson, was returning from Bois Blanc with about twenty-five hundred Presbyterian Sunday school picnickers cramming its decks. The steamer's crew saw the danger and turned the ship in time to avoid a collision.

The *Mitchell* was a few hundred feet away, following the *Columbia* down stream. Smoke from the *Columbia's* stack drifted like fog over the river, temporarily hiding the schooner from the *Mitchell's* officers. When the *Schuette* suddenly emerged through the smoke, the steamer was dead ahead. The two ships crashed bow-on. The *Schuette's* wooden hull collapsed like an egg shell, sending the coal-laden ship on a nose-dive to the bottom of the river. The crew had just enough time to get away in the ship's life boat.

The *Schuette* was never salvaged. Pieces of the wreck still lie on the bottom of the river. Because it was a menace to passing ships, the wreck was broken up by dynamite abut a month after the accident.

Sources:

Detroit Free Press, "Schooner Struck by Freighter and Sinks," July 3, 1909, news clipping, Institute for Great Lakes Research, Bowling Green State University, Perrysburg, OH.

Toledo Blade, "Sinking of Boat Averts Disaster," July 3, 1909, news clipping, Institute for Great Lakes Research, Perrysburg, OH.

On The Rocks

Schooners and other sailing vessels were sometimes driven on the rocks where their wooden hulls were smashed by the great storms that swept the lakes. Fragments of these lost ships still can be found in the shifting sands.

Canadian Heroine Abigail Becker

Many fine ships have gone to wreck off Lake Erie's notorious Long Point, a twenty-mile-long stretch of land mass jutting southeast from Port Rowan, Ontario. The stories about the wrecks in this area are legend. Among the best is a tale about Abigail Becker, who, at age twenty-three, single handily saved the crew of the wrecked schooner *Conductor* during a November gale in 1854.

Abigail was described as a "well-knit" woman of rugged pioneer stock who took up residence with her husband, Jeremiah, and their two children in a shanty at the tip of Long Point. Jeremiah Becker was a hunter and trapper who chose to live in the wilderness near his trap lines. At the time of the *Conductor* disaster, he was away on a trip to the nearest Canadian town to sell pelts and to stock up on supplies for the winter.

The *Conductor,* under command of Capt. Henry Hackett, was carrying ten thousand bushels of corn from Amherstburg to Toronto. The ship was blown off course in the storm and grounded on the point during the early morning hours of November 24. The gale was so terrible the sails from the three-master were torn away and the life boat was ripped from its davits. The Beckers discovered the wreck lying about three hundred feet offshore when they awoke at daybreak. The ship was tilted at a strange angle and waves from the still-raging storm were rolling relentlessly over its decks. It was obvious that in time the vessel would be torn asunder by the lashing it was taking. Sailors could be seen hanging in the ship's rigging.

Mrs. Becker knew the men needed to be rescued or they would perish, but how was she going to do it? She didn't even have a row boat with which to try to reach the wreck. Even if she had such a boat, how could she hope to survive in the surf? With her children's help, her first action was to build a large bonfire on the beach. The fire served as a signal to the sailors that their plight was known and that help was coming. Next she spent most of the day building a raft. One account said she used several large bed posts, possibly from the beds in the Becker home. In the meantime, the storm continued to rage without any sign of letting up. By 3:00 PM the raft was finished. The surf was still dangerously high but Becker wanted to get the stranded sailors off the wreck before nightfall if possible. She signaled the men, inviting them to try to swim to shore while she came halfway to reach them on her makeshift raft. To show her sincerity, Abigail waded boldly out in the frigid water, using the raft as a support against the power of the waves.

Captain Hackett made the first try. Even though he was weak from the hours that he spent clinging to the ropes, Hackett dropped into the frothing surf and started swimming toward the little raft. He got close enough for the woman to snag him and then pull him to shore. He stumbled ashore exhausted but alive. Hackett insisted on going back in the water with Becker to help when a second sailor made the long swim. He collapsed and Becker had to pull both men out of the water at the same time. For the rest of the day, Becker continued to wade into the freezing surf, grasping struggling bodies one-by-one. By nightfall all but the ship's cook, Jeremiah Sawyer, were safe and warm inside the Becker cabin. Sawyer spent a terrible night alone on the wreck. Becker maintained her vigil, keeping the bonfire going on the beach to let him know that he was not forgotten. By the next morning the storm was starting to let up. Sawyer was pulled from the wreck and he was still alive.

When the story of her deeds became known, Abigail Becker was a national heroine. Local merchants gave her money. The Life-Saving Benevolent Association of Canada awarded her a gold medal. The Canadian government gave her a one-hundred-acre farm near Port Rowan. England's Queen Victoria sent a letter, thanking her for her accomplishment. One account said the queen's gift also included a Bible.

Sources:

Detroit Daily Free Press, "The Schooner *Conductor* Wrecked," Dec. 3, 1854, from news clipping lakes history file, Detroit Public Library, Detroit, Mich.

Detroit Free Press, anniversary story about the *Conductor* sinking, Nov. 29, 1954, from microfilm rolls, State Library of Michigan, Lansing, Mich.

Historical data about the wreck of the *Conductor*, from the Fort Malden National Historic Park Museum, Amherstburg, Ont.

Morrison, Dr. Neil F., "The Abigail Becker Story," as it appeared in the *Erie Sunday Times*, Sept. 11, 1955, news clipping history file, Erie Public Library, Erie, Pa.

*Artist's concept of the **Tanner** shows the vessel rigged as a barkentine, with square sails on the foremast. The ship wrecked near Milwaukee during a storm in 1875. Courtesy Institute for Great Lakes Research.*

Watching the Captain Drown

The water from Lake Michigan was still dripping from the hair of Charles P. Anderson, first mate of the wrecked bark *Tanner* when a reporter for the *Milwaukee Commercial Times* caught up with him. Anderson, a large man whose bulging muscles danced as he pulled a warm and dry cardigan over his head, was obviously annoyed, but he handled this unexpected intrusion in the same stoic way he took care of everything in his world . . . head on. The fact that he had just been snatched from the jaws of death after his ship went aground and broke up near Milwaukee during a fierce autumn gale made him a brief celebrity and he was being asked to tell his story. Because he cooperated, the wreck of the *Tanner* remains among the surviving horror stories about the fate of Great Lakes sailing ships.

The *Tanner* was one of several ships lost in the storm that swept the lakes on September 10, 1875. Unlike some of the other disasters of the day, nine of the bark's crew members survived. Only the master, Capt. M. D. Howard, was drowned. Anderson told how that happened. He said the ship sailed that evening from Milwaukee with its holds filled with twenty-two thousand bushels of wheat bound for Buffalo, New York. The storm struck at about 8:00 PM when the *Tanner* was only three miles out of port. Ominous black clouds with lightning and thunder rolled down from the north. Howard ordered all hands to reef sails and drop anchors. From the way the clouds were rolling, he expected violent wind and proceeded to take every precaution to protect the ship. The storm was approaching too fast for him to consider turning the vessel around and racing back into the harbor.

As expected, the tempest arrived with great power and wrath. The *Tanner* endured the onslaught well at first. The storm grew in intensity as the evening hours passed. The wind shifted to the northeast and blew a full gale. About midnight the waves, which had been washing over the decks, increased in force until the ship's anchors dragged. The ship drifted on the rocks about a quarter-mile south of the Milwaukee harbor at about 4:00 AM. Anderson said the sailors found no haven in the ship, which by then was being buried under mountain high waves. To escape they climbed into the rigging, lashing themselves to the masts and cross trees, hoping to survive until the storm died down and help arrived.

Anderson said he was among the sailors hanging in the rigging that black night. He said he watched in disbelief as James Hansen, the ship's cook, pealed off his clothing and make a crazy effort to swim to shore. "He swam well and did not have far to reach the beach," he said. Hansen made it. Watching from shore was Capt. Theodore Saveland, who waded into the surf with the help of some nearby railroad equipment and grabbed the plucky swimmer before he drowned.

Captain Howard didn't fare was well. "The captain was hanging on just below me," continued Anderson. "I saw him last between eight and nine o'clock. He complained of being very cold and numb. We were both wet to the skin. It was impossible to reach us with a boat as the waves were rolling full over the rigging. The captain said 'Charlie, we can't hold on here much longer. I am going to try and make shore.' I advised him not to do it, for I thought he was too cold to swim.

At that moment he threw himself from the mast and disappeared in the water. I saw him rise once and I tried to catch his shoulder, but without success. The waves washed him under and he was drowned."

Had Howard remained aboard the wreck, he probably would have been saved with the other members of the *Tanner's* crew. Rescue was only about an hour away. Even though the storm continued to blow, the tugs *J. B. Merrill* and *J. J. Hagerman,* and the U.S. Revenue Cutter *Andrew Johnson* all came out that morning and took the sailors off. Anderson said the *Merrill* pulled up close and threw a rope, which the men collectively tied themselves to. In that way, they were all pulled half swimming and half drowned to the deck of a waiting scow. It was a daring rescue that saved the lives of the eight trapped sailors. "I could not have held on much longer," admitted Anderson.

Sources:

     Chicago Inter Ocean, Chicago, Ill., news stories Sept. 11, 12, 13, 14, and 16, 1875, news clips, Institute for Great Lakes Research, Perrysburg, O.

     Cleveland Herald, Cleveland, O., news stories Sept. 13, 14 and 15, news clips, Institute for Great Lakes Research, Perrysburg, O.

     Institute for Great Lakes Research, Perrysburg, O., master data sheets.

Wreck of the *Berlin*

The three-masted schooner *Berlin* was lost on Lake Huron's rocky coast at Pointe aux Barques, Michigan. Four sailors died in the wreck which happened during a wild winter gale on November 6, 1877. The *Berlin,* under the command of Capt. A. M. Johnson of Buffalo, was blown off course in the night and it slammed into a sunken reef about one mile offshore. The wooden hulled ship was in immediate peril because it broached as it struck, allowing a broadside assault from the seas. Captain Johnson knew that without a miracle, the ship would break up and he and his crew stood little chance of reaching shore alive.

The captain went about trying to save his ship with reckless determination. The fact that he owned the twenty-two-year-old vessel might have generated his zeal. He and some of the crew members stood fast against the onslaught of the great seas and raging wind as they tried to lighten the ship by jettisoning the deck load of limestone. Sometimes vessels could be worked free by removing cargo. A lighter ship rides higher in the water. As they struggled with the heavy rock, Captain Johnson and two other men were swept overboard to drown. After that, the captain's son, Richard Johnson, and sailors Martin Oleson and Charles Hanson, all of Buffalo, gave up. They agreed that remaining on the sea ravaged deck was suicide. The three sailors scrambled into the ship's rigging and hung there, clinging for their lives, as the storm raged around them for the rest of the night.

The next morning the wreck was spotted by people on shore and word was sent to the life savers at Huron City, about nine miles away. The life savers, under Capt. Charles McDonald, reached the wreck at about 3:00 PM. By then, only Oleson and Hanson remained alive. Johnson's frozen body had to be cut away from the ropes that lashed him to the mast. The *Berlin* broke up before the storm abated.

Sources:
> *Chicago Inter Ocean,* "Loss of the *Berlin*," Nov. 14, 1877, news clipping, Institute for Great Lakes Research, Perrysburg, O.
> *Detroit Free Press,* " Schooner *Berlin* Driven on a Reef," Nov. 13, and "The Captain and Crew of the Ill-Fated *Berlin*," Nov. 14, 1877, microfilm rolls, State Library of Michigan, Lansing, Mich.

Chaos at Sand Beach

The Army Corps of Engineers was in the process of building what was to be called the largest man-made harbor in the world at Sand Beach, the old name for Harbor Beach, Michigan, in 1879. Only a part of the mile-wide stone breakwater was in place on November 19 when the area got hit by a freak storm that raised such havoc that seven ships were beached or sunk and five sailors were drowned. The disaster was of such scale that it might have changed the minds of

*The schooner-barge **Emma C. Hutchinson,** foreground, was one of seven vessels left sunk or run aground after a freak storm ravaged the boats moored at Sand Beach in 1879. Courtesy Institute for Great Lakes Research.*

some of the town's civic leaders, who were opposed to the harbor construction project. The storm bore down from the north-northwest with a vengeance. As it gained in strength, boats of all size and description made their way into the harbor, hoping to find shelter behind the stone breakwaters and pier. By nightfall, an estimated seventy-five vessels were moored and anchored there. Their masts appeared like a forest of bare trees, locked in a wild and chaotic dance as the wind and seas caused the ships to roll.

That night the storm grew even stronger and it began to snow. The gale hammered at the harbor through its open, uncompleted gap, and the anchored fleet found little or no shelter. Any ship not securely tied to the pier soon found itself in serious trouble. Anchors dragged. Drifting hulls began to slam into each other. Vessels drifted into the shallow harbor mud. Crews chose to scuttle their boats to keep them from pounding to pieces in the surf. A correspondent for the *Port Huron Weekly Times* wrote that many ships were scattered by the gale, and their masters chose to put back into open water rather than be wrecked on the beach.

By the next morning the steamer *J. R. Whiting,* loaded with coal, and the schooner-barge *Emma C. Hutchinson* were sunk in eighteen feet of water. The steamer *Salina* was aground along with its consorts, *F. B. Gardner, William Rayner, Prairie State* and *Jarvis Wells.* Yet another schooner, the *Bahama,* which also had been in tow behind the *Whiting,* was sunk after striking a rock. Five sailors from the *Prairie State* and *Jarvis Wells* were drowned when a life boat they were using to try to get to shore capsized. Among the dead were William Little and Rogert Ogden, both of Saginaw, Michigan, John Woods, of London, Ontario, and two other sailors whose identities were undisclosed.

Sailors on all the boats found themselves in a desperate situation as the seas rolled over their vessels, smashing windows, railings and cabins and flooding every nook and corner. After the *Bahama* sank on a large boulder, which put a hole in the hull, the crew spent the night standing on a board propped between the top of the rock and a chair so they could be out of the water while still sheltered from the storm.

One would-be rescuer, G. F. Kaumier of Sand Beach, was on the pier, attempting to climb aboard the tug *George Hand,* when a large wave washed him off the pier. He landed, unharmed, on the deck of the nearby barge *Huron City.* A rescue crew trying to reach the sailors on the *Rayner* had to turn back on the first try because the breakers smashed the life boat's rudder. A second attempt was successful and the *Rayner's* crew was successfully brought ashore.

The schooner *Hathaway* was involved in a collision with the schooner *Maumee Valley* off Sand Beach that night. Neither vessel was sunk but both were damaged in the crash. Both vessels survived the gale. The *Hathaway* limped down the St. Clair River and docked at Port Huron the next day.

Source:
        Port Huron Weekly Times, "Marine News," Nov. 27, 1879, news clippings, Institute for Great Lakes Research, Perrysburg, Mi.

Escape from Disaster

That the crew of the schooner *George W. Holt* came out of it alive was considered miraculous to the people of Port Austin, Michigan. They watched helplessly from shore the evening of July 19, 1880 as the ship, driven by a wild summer storm, struck the dreaded Port Austin Reef and then fell apart before their eyes. Within an hour after the ship grounded, nothing more could be seen of it. Nobody thought there would be survivors. The next morning people searched the mass of jangled spars, ropes and broken planks littering about two miles of the shore, looking for bodies that were not there. Then the word came that the crew was safe at the nearby light-house.

The *Holt,* with Capt. B. H. Hoose at the helm, was carrying five hundred and thirty-three tons of iron ore from Marquette to Detroit when it got caught in the storm on Lake Huron. The twenty-three-year-old ship, owned by Capt. Hoose and his daughter, Nettie Hoose, was one of three downbound sailing vessels in tow behind the steam barge *Iron Age.* The ship had been sold to a Detroit man and the Hoose family, including the captain's wife and a third unidentified woman, were aboard for what was supposed to have been a pleasant summer trip before the *Holt* went to its new owner.

The schooner sprung a leak in the midst of the storm. Capt. Hoose ordered his crew to man the bilge pump, but it couldn't keep up with the rising water. The storm, plus the extra drag caused by the waterlogged ship, broke the tow line somewhere off Pointe aux Barques. The gale was blowing from the northeast so Hoose raised sail and ran his ship before the wind toward Port Austin, hoping to reach that harbor before the *Holt* sank out from under him. For a while it looked as if he would make it. As the vessel approached the harbor, how-ever, Hoose either miscalculated his position, it could not be steered or the ship got blown off course. It struck the reef at 5:00 PM. Fortunately it crunched to a stop about four hun-dred feet from the lighthouse, located on the reef and about a mile off shore. As the schooner began breaking up, Hoose or-dered the lifeboat launched. The captain, his wife, daughter and their guest, plus a crew of seven sailors, got to the light-house where keeper Charles Kimball and his assistant, Charles McDonald, hoisted them to safety with ropes. The captain's wife was the only casualty. She dislocated an arm while being lifted to the lighthouse pier. The crew and passengers of the *Holt* were forced to stay in the lighthouse for two days until the storm abated.

Sources:
> *Cleveland Herald,* "Loss of the *G. W. Holt,*" July 22, 1880, news clippings, Institute for Great Lakes Research, Perrysburg, O.
> *Huron County News,* Port Austin, Mi., July 29, 1880, microfilm rolls, Huron County Library, Bad Axe, Mi.
> *Huron Times,* Sand Beach, Mi., July 22, 1880, bound newspapers, city clerk's office, Harbor Beach, Mi.

Saving the Cook

If there was a woman aboard a Great Lakes ship in 1880, she was there as a guest of the captain or else she was aboard to cook for the crew. Sometimes, on the larger vessels and especially on passenger liners, women were hired to clean cabins and generally keep house. The business of running the ship was left up to the men. A sailor's life was an especially dangerous occupation in those times. It was no easier or safer for the women. In fact, many stories were told about how the cook was left behind on a grounded ship to die while all of the men swam for shore. If there was one death, it often was the female cook or steward that was lost. If she didn't go down with the ship, get trapped below deck when the vessel capsized, she froze to death in frigid seas while strapped to the mast.

There were exceptions. When the *Cortez* wrecked on Lake Ontario on November 12, 1880, the sailors went out of their way to save the cook. The ship went aground in a gale on the southern shore of the lake near Oswego, New York. Crew member Thomas Highland of Buffalo told how the captain and crew dressed the cook in "a couple of pairs of sailor pants and blankets" before tying her in the ship's rigging to wait for a rescue. All members of the crew were hanging in the ropes over the deck when a local fishing vessel took them

*The schooner **Cortez** was wrecked when it ran on the rocks on Lake Ontario in 1880. Courtesy Institute for Great Lakes Research.*

off at dusk. Everybody survived the wreck, even the cook, who was never identified.

Highland said the *Cortez* lost its jibs and stay sails in the gale while off Port Dalhousie (the old name for St. Catherines, Ontario) and was taking on water as it blew east before the wind toward Oswego. As the stricken ship approached the coast, he said Oswego was in sight, but because of the lost sails the crew could not control its direction and the *Cortez* drifted past that port. The vessel worked its way into Mexico Bay before going aground at the extreme east end of Lake Ontario. Highland said the anchors were dropped, but they dragged. He said the ship "gradually drifted broadside shoreward. Early on Friday afternoon she struck the beach and swung round at the mercy of the waves, and finally settled in the sandy bottom about three-quarters of a mile from the shore."

Highland was critical of the Sandy Creek lifesaving station. He said the lookout there had to have seen the *Cortez* as it drifted past, its sails torn, heading for certain destruction, but no boats were sent to help. People on shore watched the drama unfold. After the ship struck, one of the local fishing tugs braved the storm to get the crew off. He said everybody remained in the rigging about four hours before help arrived. The *Cortez* broke up and was a total loss.

Source:
    Chicago Inter Ocean, "The *Cortez;* Particulars of the Disaster, from the *Oswego Palladium,*" Nov. 18, 1880, news clipping file, Institute for Great Lakes Research, Perrysburg, O.

Slamming Into an Island

Thomas O'Neil, first mate of the lost schooner *James Platt,* was still having a hard time believing that he and many of his shipmates were still among the living. The *Platt,* carrying salt from Bay City, Michigan, to Chicago, was driven aground on Lake Michigan's South Fox Island during a winter gale on November 25, 1881. Captain Henry Turner and the cook, Belma Champaigne, drowned attempting to launch the lifeboat. O'Neil and five other sailors were rescued by the local lighthouse keeper after clinging to the ice-coated wreck for two nights and a day.

O'Neil said the *Platt* left Bay City on November 18 in company with the schooners *George W. Bissell* and *Emma L. Coyne;* all three vessels under tow of the steam tug *Gladiator.* After clearing the straits, the tug left the three schooners at the north end of Lake Michigan. All set their sails and turned southward. The gale, accompanied by snow and freezing temperatures, developed out of the southwest on Friday night. Instead of trying to run against the wind and sea, Captain Turner turned his ship around and sailed northeast, hoping to find shelter behind South Manitou Island. When he realized that he was too far south, he changed course for Beaver Island. O'Neil said it was a terrible trip. He said the wind was so powerful that Turner ordered nearly all of the sails reefed, yet the *Platt* was tipped so that its lee rail was dipped under water most of the way. "It was so cold the ice was forming as every sea rolled over the bow. The rigging soon got iced up and it was impossible to handle." The snow was falling so heavily that the sailors were blinded most of the time. Then the ship's lookout shouted "Land Ho!" South Fox Island was looming up only a half mile ahead. The crew struggled to turn the ship from harm's way but it was too late. The *Platt* struck so hard that all three masts toppled. The sailors were thrown against bulkheads and knocked to the deck. In an instant the schooner was a complete wreck.

Without sails and rigging to escape to, the crew had no choice but to cling to the wreck and bear the torture of the seas as they relentlessly swept the twisted decks, keeping everybody drenched. It was so cold that everything was coated with ice. Captain Turner was convinced that his crew could not survive the night under these conditions. He tried to launch the yawl and make a run for shore. The crew attempted to lower the boat on the lee side of the wreck, with the cook, Belma Champaign and Turner aboard to help guide it into the water. The frail craft caught on the painter and tipped, spilling both Turner and Campaign into the sea to drown. The lifeboat was lost so it was impossible for the others to try again. O'Neil said it was discovered that the forecastle offered a little relief from the storm so the sailors got behind it and waited. He said some of the men were praying for deliverance.

Meanwhile, on the island, lighthouse keeper W. S. Warner was aware that a ship was in trouble offshore and he was trying to help. Warner, his son, and helper Morris Leslie tried to launch a boat that same night, but the surf was so high that the boat capsized. The three men found their way back to shore and then built a fire to let the sailors know that help was nearby. Warner said it was a long wait as the gale continued for another twenty-four hours before letting up. It was not until Sunday that Warner and his companions were able to successfully launch their boat and take off the exhausted men. By then the sailors were weak from exposure and their coats were heavily coated with ice. Amazingly, everybody was still alive. Rescued were John Cummings, John Hartney, Thomas Carey, Charles West and Edmund Larsen.

Source:
    Detroit Evening News, Dec. 6, 1881, microfilm rolls, State Library of Michigan, Lansing, Mich.

The Ship that Fell Apart

The crew of the schooner *Gallatin* felt lucky to be alive after their ship was wrecked in the midst of a Lake Erie storm on April 23, 1882. Captain E. M. Fuller of Chicago said the ship was laden with pig iron, bound from St. Ignace, Michigan, to Erie, Pennsylvania, when it developed a leak while battling the blow off Sandusky, Ohio. At first he said the ship was "leaking a little, but not so badly but that the pumps would keep her free." When near Cleveland, Fuller said the storm intensified into a full blown gale. As the schooner took more punishment, the leak got worse.

"At 1:00 AM we squared her away up the lake before the wind and kept both pumps going, but the water gained on us." Fuller said that as the ship settled deeper in the water, the seas began washing the decks from astern. That was when the *Gallatin* began coming unglued. First the seas ripped the ship's yawl from its davits. Next went the bulwarks and part of the aft cabin. "She got so much water in her that she was unmanageable, and a few minutes later she struck Chickanola Reef. The crew got into the rigging . . . and in fifteen minutes the vessel went to the bottom, going down in about fifteen feet of water. She commenced breaking up immediately, and her decks and what remained of her cabin washed away."

As the storm raged, the men hung in the ropes, worried that at any moment the masts would fall as the ship continued to turn to junk under them. They knew their chances of surviving in the churning waters were poor. The water was so cold in April that no man could expect to stay alive more than a few minutes, even if they were strong swimmers. Fuller said they could see Kelly Island in the distance, and the large steam tugs *Vulcan* and *Torrent* moored there. Nobody on the island noticed the schooner go on the reef and the tugs were never dispatched. The sailors hung in the rigging for about eight hours before the crew of the local fishing boat *Lizzie,* brought them in.

The fishermen, Capt. William Holton, C. G. Monaghan, Thomas McCormick, Arthur McCormick and "Siney" Mahony, had spent the night on Point Pelee Island waiting out the storm. They purposefully left their boat sunk offshore to keep it safe during the storm. That morning they watched the *Gallatin* come in under foresail, staysail and jib, strike the reef and start breaking up. It took the fishermen most of the day to pump their boat dry and get it underway to make the rescue. They had all seven sailors, six men and a woman, aboard and on their way to a safe harbor by 4:00 PM.

Sources:
    Detroit Free Press, "Loss of the Schooner *Gallatin*, Apr. 23, also "The Crew of the *Gallatin*," Apr. 26, 1882, microfilm rolls, State Library of Michigan, Lansing, Mich.
    Cleveland Herald, "Loss of the *Gallatin*—Sandusky Marine" Apr. 23, 1882, from news clipping file, Institute for Great Lakes Research, Perrysburg, O.

Wreck of the *Laura Bell*

Nobody will know the suffering experienced by the crew of the *Laura Belle* after the ship wrecked on Shot Point, on the rugged Lake Superior coast near Marquette, Michigan. The coal-laden schooner, under the command of Capt. Hugh Hastings, got within twelve miles of its destination before grinding to a jarring stop in the blinding, storm-tossed night of September 7, 1883. Crew member William Howell of Kingston, Ohio, was killed in the crash when he was struck on the neck by a wild swinging boom. After the accident there was nothing to do but wait for the storm to quit and help to arrive.

Waiting for help on a desolate Lake Superior reef in 1883 was torture. There was no radio with which to summon assistance. The only choice for those trapped aboard the *Laura Belle* was to hang on and hope somebody spotted them from shore or from a passing ship before death came. The storm did all that it could to destroy the wreck they were clinging to. It also prevented them from making a dash for shore. The seas carried away the lifeboat, demolished the cabins and swept away anything else not securely bolted to the deck. There was no sanctuary. To escape from the violence on the deck, the men climbed the ship's rigging, tied themselves in place, and then prayed that the masts holding them suspended overhead withstood the forces of both wind and wave. The suffering even there was unbearable. Except for the wet clothing they wore, there was no shelter from the wind and rain that buffeted their bodies. They waited there for three long days before the word got to Marquette and a tug was sent. By then there was little left of the wreck and the men were nearly perished from hunger and exhaustion. Some were so weak they had to be carried ashore. People marveled that all still lived.

Capt. Hastings said the gale was so violent it damaged the ship's rudder, leaving the schooner to the mercy of the wind. When the *Laura Belle* struck the reef, the crash knocked two large holes in the hull and wedged the vessel so tightly among the rocks that he knew there would be no hope of ever saving it. Even the cargo of six hundred tons of coal, assigned to the Marquette & Ontonagon Railroad in Marquette, was lost.

A Marquette news reporter described the wreck in a story in the *Detroit Free Press* on September 13: "She lies with her head on a rocky shoal in twelve feet of water about eighty rods from shore. A large boulder lies under the middle of her and humps her up about four feet. Her bottom must be gone for the coal has sunk three feet. Her starboard side is gone, her stern is all open and she is twisted out of shape. The water washes over her decks and the first northwest wind will break her to pieces." The schooner was owned by Capt. Hastings and Charles Edwards, of Milan, Ohio. It was built at Toledo in 1870.

Sources:
> *Detroit Free Press,* "Wreck News from Marquette," Sept. 13, 1883, microfilm rolls, State Library of Michigan, Lansing, Michigan.
> *Cleveland Herald,* "The Schooner *Laura Bell* Lost," and "The *Laura Bell* Disaster," Sept. 11 and 12, 1883, news clipping file, Institute for Great Lakes Research, Perrysburg, O.

Hiding in the Forecastle

When a summer storm drove the Canadian schooner *Elgin* aground near Racine, Wisconsin on Sunday, August 2, 1885, the crew had a rare chance to seek refuge in the forecastle until the storm abated two days later. The ship went on bow first and stopped so that the seas, driven by a northeast gale, assaulted the stern, never getting enough force to tear the forward cabin away from the main deck. The ship's master, a man named Lawson, said the *Elgin* took a pounding for a while until the sailors scuttled the hull. Then it settled on a sandy bottom and took the seas without any further threat to the ship or the men trapped on its decks.

Captain Lawson said the *Elgin* was sailing southwest before the wind across Lake Michigan toward Chicago with a load of cedar lumber when it struck the shore five miles north of Racine Point at about 9:00 PM. At first he said he was afraid that the ship would break up under the onslaught of the waves. After the holds were flooded, however, the *Elgin* settled and the men were surprised to find that they could shelter in the cabin instead of choosing the traditionally prescribed method of escape for seafaring sailors in that period. That was climbing into the rigging and hanging in the ropes until help came. Even though they were sheltered, the cabin was not a comfortable place to wait. During the night the compartments flooded regularly. The sailors were forced to stand in water much of the time. Some of the men built swinging cots, which they hung from the cabin roof and tried to sleep. Everybody was cold and wet.

Monday morning came and the crew greeted the day with high hopes of escape. As the hours passed, it became apparent that help would not be coming. A heavy fog wrapped around them like a blanket, preventing passing ships or the people on shore from spotting the wreck. The seas remained so high that attempting to reach shore in the life boat seemed foolhardy. The sailors remained on the wreck for another full day. On Monday night, the seas were still high, but Lawson was determined not to spend another night in the forecastle. He ordered the lifeboat launched, and the sailors pulled for shore, taking the surf with great peril. They made it. There they found themselves on barren shores. They walked five miles south to Racine before finding shelter.

There is evidence that the *Elgin* was raised and repaired. There were two Canadian based schooners with the names *Elgin* sailing the lakes in 1885. Both vessels were still in commission the following year. One of them was sold and its name was changed to *Oakland* in 1885.

Source:
Beers, J. H. & Co., History of the Great Lakes Illustrated, Vol. II, Chicago, 1899.

Cleveland Leader, "The Schooner *Elgin,*" Aug. 7, 1885, news clipping, Institute for Great Lakes Research, Perrysburg, O.

Wreck of the *O. B. Bond*

Capt. Peter Lefevre lost his ship on Lake Erie after a sudden squall laid it almost on its side and a cargo of grain shifted. The schooner *O. B. Bond* was loaded with wheat, sailing from Detroit to Buffalo, when the accident happened on the afternoon of Thursday, October 14, 1886. Lefevre said the ship was sailing under reefed lower sails against a brisk southerly wind when he watched an evil appearing black cloud full of wind and fury whipping across the lake from the west. Even though he saw it coming and took every precaution, Lefevre said "the squall rolled her over into the south sea and her cargo shifted so badly that she would not steer. Soon after the vessel was driven ashore about four miles above Rondau light."

The *Bond* remained in its strange, semi-capsized position on its port side after it struck the shore. There, Lefevre said, the seas swept the decks, buffeting the vessel mercilessly. The wreck was located too far from dry land for the crew to escape while the storm continued to blow. The sailors first climbed into the rigging around the main mast, but after a while, Lefevre began to suspect that this mast was weakened and would not stand much longer against the pounding. He said he told the others about his fears and persuaded all but one sailor to climb from the main to the foremast rigging. Lefevre, the cook and three sailors got on the crosstrees, while Patrick Ryan, the ship's mate, and a sailor named James Hughes stayed in the ratlines below the trucks. The main mast did fall, carrying the single sailor into the water with it. On its way down, the spar struck the fore-rigging, knocking both Hughes and Ryan off. They disappeared and were never seen again. Lefevre said the sailor who rode the main mast over later climbed back on the deck and into the fore-rigging. The man said his foot became tangled with the ropes after he fell in the lake, and he had to use his knife to cut his boot away to free himself.

The survivors held on for about twenty-four hours until the storm abated enough for rescuers to bring a skiff out to the wreck and take them off. By then the *Bond* was a total wreck. Its cabins were swept away by the seas, the deck was warped, the grain was wet and swelling, the deck beams were cracked from the pressure. The foremast fell on Sunday morning.

The *Bond* appeared to be destined for destruction that year. A few months earlier the ship sustained extensive damage when it struck the pier at Dalhousie, Ontario. After it was written off by insurance companies as a constructive total loss, Captain Lefevre purchased the wreck and had it completely rebuilt. It was on its second trip after leaving dry dock when it was destroyed on Lake Erie.

Sources:
Detroit Free Press, "Storm-Beaten Mariners," Oct. 19, 1886, and "Marine News," Oct. 18, 1886, microfilm rolls, State Library of Michigan, Lansing, Mich.
Detroit Post and Tribune, "The Wreck of the O. B. Bond," Oct. 19, 1886, microfilm rolls, State Library of Michigan, Lansing, Mich.
Duluth Daily Tribune, "The Loss of the O. B. Bond," Oct. 21, 1886, news clipping, Institute for Great Lakes Research, Perrysburg, O.

*Anchor and chain from the lost schooner **Emerald** stand as a silent memorial near Kewaunee, Wisconsin, to the lost ships and men of the Great Lakes. Courtesy Institute for Great Lakes Research.*

Two Lost Barges

The anchor and chain from the wrecked schooner *Emerald* stand mounted in concrete on a bluff near Kewaunee, Wisconsin. They are a memorial to eight sailors who died when their ships were lost near that spot during a Lake Michigan gale on November 17, 1886. The storm raged for three days. By the time it was over, nearly fifty lives were lost and thirty-five lake vessels were either sunk or driven ashore.

The *Emerald* and *Florence M. Dickinson* were part of a string of four coal-laden barges in tow to Milwaukee behind the tug *Chief Justice Field.* Also in the tow were the barges *Lily May* and *G. W. Bissell.* A marine writer for the *Chicago Inter Ocean* later said all four vessels were worn out wooden-hulled and square-built schooners, long past their prime, and probably in no condition to battle the northeaster that struck them. The storm developed early in the morning and the *Field* began drifting off its course. As the seas built, the *Dickinson* was the first to get in trouble. The old barge sprang a leak, began pulling hard and broke its tow line. Capt. Thomas Robinson ordered canvas raised and the crew tried to sail before the wind into nearby Kewaunee harbor. A sailing ship scudding before a wind has no brakes. When a mistake is made under severe conditions such as the *Dickinson* was experiencing, there is no way to fix it. As the barge raced toward the piers at Kewaunee, a large wave turned the ship to starboard, the wheelsman overcorrected and the schooner swept past the north breakwater, crashing into a large rock. Within minutes the *Dickinson* was going to pieces in the surf. The lifeboat was swept away by a wave before it could be launched. Robinson and four other members of the crew swam to the breakwater where they were pulled to safety. Sailors Jerry Jeru and Arthur Prevo, both of Green Bay, and the cook, Mary Walters of Buffalo, stayed aboard the wreck and perished there. They were last seen clinging to the mast when it collapsed. Within two hours the old barge was completely broken into a scattering of cracked boards and kindling along the beach.

Meanwhile, the three remaining barges also were battling the storm from just offshore. The *Field* cut the tow lines and ran for shelter at Manitowoc. The barges had their anchors down and were trying to ride out the storm in deep water. The *Emerald's* anchor failed to hold and the ship began following the *Dickinson* toward the rocks. Capt. A. Gorman of Marine City, Michigan, raised distress signals and they were seen by people ashore. Word was sent to the lifesavers at Two Rivers and Sturgeon Bay. Because of the press of other ships in distress that morning, help did not arrive. The *Emerald* came ashore about a half mile south of the pier about 11:00 AM and began breaking up.

The people of Kewaunee watched helplessly as the six members of the doomed schooner's crew, five men and a woman, launched the lifeboat and it immediately capsized. Only William Condrey, the mate, made it to shore alive. He was clinging to an oar when he reached shallow water where helping hands dragged him to safety. Drowned from the *Emerald* were Captain Gorman, brothers Mike and Louis Pontak, William Alberta, all of Green Bay, Wisconsin, and the cook, Maggie Clark of Milwaukee.

Sources:

    Chicago Inter Ocean "Eight Lives Lost," and "The Gale's Havoc," Nov. 18 and 19, 1886, news clippings, Institute for Great Lakes Research, Perrysburg, O.

    Fon du Lac Daily Reporter, Fon du Lac, Wis., "Wrecks on the Lake," Nov. 18, 1886, news clipping, Institute for Great Lakes Research, Perrysburg, O.

The Killer Storms of '86

The vessels still working late in November 1886, got caught in a string of killer winter storms that brought sixty-mile-per-hour winds, blinding snow and zero degree temperatures. The gales began on November 17 and continued on into December with such stark power they incapacitated sailors, brought mountainous seas that drove ships off their course, and coated decks, ropes and sails with so much ice that vessels were out of control. The storms followed one another like freight cars and each blow took such a broad swath that sailors were in trouble on every end of the lakes. By the time it was over two weeks later, the coasts from Chicago to Kingston were strewn with the remains of wrecked and sunken ships. Many of the sailors who survived were left incapacitated from severe frostbite of their hands and feet. Horror stories abounded. A few are recorded here:

The *Ariadne* Disaster

The people of Oswego, New York, were concerned for the safety of the crews of several vessels known to be standing off that Lake Ontario harbor as a storm blasted the area on December 1. In the evening, when the wind shifted from the southwest to west and the storm intensified, rockets were fired by the life saving crew from the piers and large bonfires were kept burning by townspeople to guide the ships into port through the blinding snowstorm. About 8:00 PM the shadow of a crippled schooner was observed drifting past the harbor. The ship's mainmast was toppled and the crew was flying signals of distress. A tugboat steamed out to try to bring the schooner in, but when it reached the gap in the breakwater where the storm struck it with full force, the tug was nearly swamped by the seas and was forced to turn back. The crew reported the ship to be the schooner *Ariadne,* laden with barley and bound to Oswego from Toronto, Ontario.

Meanwhile, aboard the crippled vessel, the crew was actively trying to save the ship and themselves. The men slid and crawled across the ice sheathed decks, laboring to cut away the mass of ropes, pulleys and broken lumber that once was the ship's main mast. All of this lay broken in a jumbled mess over one side of the ship. It was floating like a giant sea anchor and making it impossible to steer the vessel to a safe place. By the time this was cut away the *Ariadne* was blown far beyond Oswego's harbor, and was broached against the seas somewhere off Mexico Bay. Without a good harbor ahead of him, and with both wind and sea blowing the ship directly toward the rocks at the east end of the bay, Capt. Hugh McKay knew he didn't have much of a chance of saving his ship. He didn't give up. The crew jury-rigged a sail against the stump of the main mast and gained some control of the ship. The *Ariadne* still couldn't turn against the storm. With nothing to head-off the inevitable, the vessel went on a reef about 3:00 AM about twenty miles east of Oswego.

At dawn the farmers on shore discovered the wreck and saw the sailors lashed to the rigging around the forward mast. They wanted to send a rescue boat but the gale was still raging and there were no suitable boats in the area. Word was sent to the Oswego life saving station nine miles away. Because of the heavy snow and serious drifting, travel was slow. It was nearly noon before a lifeboat arrived on a horse-drawn wagon. By then the schooner was pounding to pieces. Wreckage, including a portion of the ship's stern, had already drifted ashore. It was obvious that the men still clinging to what was left of the wreck were suffering and some wondered if they could still be alive. Then there was another delay. The lifesavers found that the surf was too high to safely launch the lifeboat. A mortar and breeches buoy was sent for. It was after 3:00 PM when this apparatus arrived. By then, the only part of the wreck still visible from shore was the bow, and the bodies of only three sailors could be seen. The others, including Captain McKay, had fallen away to perish in the surf.

The mortar was fired and a life line was shot across the wreck. At first, nothing happened. It appeared that all of the men had perished on the *Ariadne*. But then, with what had to have been sheer determination, one of the men started to move. He struggled, obviously handicapped by frozen hands, to untie the ice-coated ropes that held him to the rigging. Then he slowly climbed down to the deck, where he successfully tied the rope around the spar. The people watching from shore moaned in unison as a large wave swept the wreck and the man's form disappeared. After securing the rope that could have saved him, he had been swept overboard. There was an unexpected murmur in the crowd. Suddenly people cheered when they saw that he was still alive and fighting. They saw him as he grasped a piece of floating wreckage and held on until it washed ashore. He was still alive when the people pulled him out of the surf. His work with the life line was successful. It held and the lifesavers soon had the breeches buoy in service and were aboard the wreck to bring the other two men in. The sailors were both unconscious and their limbs badly frozen. Two other frozen bodies were found on the wreck. One of them, Sutherland McKay, the captain's father, was lashed to the capstan and the other was found huddled in the forecastle.

Aboard the *Ray S. Farr*

The schooner *Ray S. Farr* had just arrived at Chicago harbor, after the completion of a trip across Lake Michigan from Muskegon, Michigan, with a load of slab wood, when the storm came. The vessel was tracking behind the schooner *Lake Forest* and had almost reached the Chicago River when the wind struck from the northwest and blew if off course. Some sailors said Captain Granzo made a mistake when he didn't drop his anchors immediately and wait for assistance from a tug. After that, Granzo was concerned about keeping his ship out of danger as the gale blew it south along the coast. His first thoughts were of finding another safe anchorage. By the time the *Farr* was off South Chicago, the storm was so intense he realized he was never going to sail successfully against the wind and reach a port on the west side of the lake. His decision was to steer southeast with the gale at his stern and beach the ship near Michigan City, Indiana.

It was a terrible trip. The wind whipped up mountain high seas that were dashing the schooner with a freezing spray that built a coat of ice on everything. The temperature dropped to eleven degrees Fahrenheit and the men complained that they couldn't stand for more than a few minutes on the deck without freezing their limbs. Captain Granzo seemed to generate super human strength. He remained on the deck for most of the trip. As the *Farr* approached the shore, he climbed up in the icy wire rigging to act as lookout, shouting orders to the sailors below him on the deck. He later was found to have frozen his nose, ears, fingers and toes. The *Farr* hit the beach at 2:30 PM, about seven miles north of Michigan City. The half frozen crew then attempted to launch the lifeboat, only to have it strike a block of floating ice and swamp. With great effort the six men managed to get the boat refloated again, then crawl into it and make their way through a field of floating ice to the shore. The schooner was destroyed by the ice.

Drifting Lumber Barges

The steam barge *Nashua* had the lumber-laden schooners *Lillie Parsons, Potomac* and *Annie Vought* in tow on Lake Erie when the storm developed. The four tired old wooden-hulled barges battled high winds, blinding snow and heavy seas together until the tow lines to the *Potomac* and *Vought* parted about 6:00 PM. Captain Hamilton, master of the *Nashua*, said the storm was so terrible it was impossible to turn around and try to recover the lost schooners. He said he continued on toward Buffalo with the *Parsons* still in tow. Six hours later, the *Parsons* also broke loose and the *Nashua* continued on alone. Hamilton said the seas were so high that at times water was pouring down the steamer's smoke stack.

The schooners all raised sail and rode before the wind, making their way through the storm in an easterly direction toward Buffalo. The *Parsons* and *Vought* were sighted about noon the next day and harbor tugs steamed out to meet them. The *Edward Fiske* got a line to the *Vought* and brought the barge in without any trouble. The tug *E. C. Maytham* found the *Parsons* anchored off Windmill Point, about six miles above the breakwater, and after two tries, got a hawser attached. This vessel also was towed safely into port. But where was the *Potomac*? The tug *Anna P. Dorr* found it broached in the seas, its rudder smashed. The schooner's anchors were dragging and the *Potomac* was drifting helplessly toward Rose's

Reef off the Ontario coast. The *Dorr's* crew worked against the storm and over ice-coated decks to get a hawser connected to the endangered *Potomac,* only to see the line break the moment the tug began to pull the drifting barge against the gale. A second cable was connected, but it also snapped.

The *Dorr's* master, Capt. William H. Hazen, returned to Buffalo with full steam up to secure yet a third and heavier hawser, then returned through the storm where it was also made fast, even as the *Potomac's* wooden hull was beginning to strike the rocks. As they battled against time to save the schooner, the men aboard both vessels suffered extreme hardship. Many of the sailors experienced frostbite on their hands and ears. There was a constant danger of someone slipping on the ice-sheeted decks and falling overboard. The last hawser held, but as the *Dorr* pulled, it was discovered that the *Potomac's* damaged rudder was twisted to one side, making it impossible for the vessel to be steered in a straight line behind the tug. The schooner had to be pulled almost sideways to Buffalo. When they arrived, both vessels were coated with about three inches of ice.

Wreck of the *William Jones*

Captain David Dall leaned back in his chair with a grin on his weather wrinkled face. A reporter from the *Chicago Inter Ocean* was at his South Water Street home, asking about the wreck of his ship, the schooner *William Jones* at Point Sable, and Dall had a story to tell. After years of seafaring, there was nothing Captain Dall enjoyed more than spinning yarns. And this was a good one. Even though his son, Captain J. H. Dall had been the master of the *Jones,* as owner of the ship, the senior Captain Dall had been along for the trip and from the way he embellished his story, he had stood the quarter deck with his son and never missed a moment of what was going on. He even joked that he had a good time. "I know some people, however, who would call it a very tough time.

"The *William Jones* left Chicago Tuesday a week ago," he began. "She had good sailing until Wednesday night between nine and ten o'clock when the gale struck us with full force. We attempted to make White Lake when the flying jibs gave away and also the cleat. This compelled us to put back into the lake where we were pounded in a lively manner by the sea, which was running mountains high. We laid to the westward and then put about to the south'ard, but fetched nothing, when we again put for White Lake. This was Thursday afternoon. Our headstays had parted in the meantime and the heaviest of the sea, which was running from the south'ard, forced us to again put on the west tack. At sunset Thursday evening, nearly twenty-four hours after the gale had struck us, it was still blowing great guns. The snow was blinding and the weather very cold. The sails could not be handled as the hoops were frozen to the masts and every rope was three times its usual thickness with ice.

"At nine-thirty o'clock that evening it had cleared up, and we sighted Ludington, but owing to the terrible seas astern we were afraid to approach the land. Two hours later we concluded to make Manistee, but could not get around Big Point Au Sable. We couldn't go south because we were too badly iced up, and there being no other alternative, when just abreast of the Point Sable lighthouse, we put the helm up and ran her ashore head-on. If we hadn't lost our head stays we would never have run her ashore, but we could carry no canvas excepting the mainsail, and that would not keep us from drifting." The *Jones* struck about midnight. "During the night the sea worked us up until the morning found us lying almost dry, broadside to. We had plenty of tarpaulin and the first thing we did when the gale struck us was to cover the skylight of the cabin, and the result was we didn't get a drop of water in it. Our cook stove capsized early in the storm and we had to go without cooked food, but when we were beached the stove was righted and a hot meal enjoyed."

The Point Sable life savers saw the ship go ashore and began preparing to risk the storm to bring the sailors on its decks to safety. Captain Dall, however, said he didn't think they needed help. "We signaled them that we were in no danger, but they trundled their heavy gun carriage a mile through the sand and threw a life line over our rigging. By the time our crew was ready to go ashore the life-savers had built a rousing bonfire on the beach."

The *Jones* was salvaged.

Sources:

Beers, J. H. & Co., History of the Great Lakes Illustrated, Volume I, Chicago, 1899.

Chicago Inter Ocean, Nov. 20-Dec. 4 issues, news clippings, Institute for Great Lakes Research, Perrysburg, O.

Detroit Free Press, Nov. 20-Dec. 4 issues, news clippings, Institute for Great Lakes Research, Perrysburg, O.

The *Presto* Wreck

After forty long years of service, the schooner *Presto* came to a violent and unexpected end when a squall drove it to destruction on the rocky coast of Lake Huron, near the north breakwater at Harbor Beach, on October 16, 1897. The ship was traveling empty from Detroit to Alpena to pick up a cargo when the accident happened. Captain Van Camp thought the weather appeared threatening so he was steering the schooner toward the protective walls of the harbor. The *Presto* was approaching from the northeast, aiming for the north gap in the mile-wide chain of stone and concrete breakwaters, when the squall struck. The schooner was blown off its course, and it went aground.

Harbor Beach life savers saw the *Presto* strike and sent a life boat. The boat was followed by two harbor tugs, the *Thomas Scott* and *Arthur Jones.* The tugs attached hawsers and tried to pull the stranded schooner free. It wouldn't budge. Even as they worked, the rising seas pounded the empty ship, driving it farther into the rocks with hammering precision. Within hours the *Presto's* hull was broken and the ship was full of water. Before the day was out, the *Presto* was declared a wreck. The crew was brought into the harbor and returned to Detroit on the next train. The next week, workers stripped the wreck of its sails and gear. The hull was left to break up and rot away with the winter storms.

*The schooner **Presto** sailed the lakes for forty years before it was dashed on the rocks at Harbor Beach, Michigan. Courtesy Institute for Great Lakes Research.*

The *Presto* had just left Detroit dry dock that week and was making its first trip after owner C. W. Chamberlain paid for extensive repair and refitting. The ship, which was built at Huron, Ohio, in 1857, measured one hundred eleven feet in length.

Sources:

    Detroit Free Press, "Schooner Wrecked at Sand Beach," Oct. 17, 1897, news clippings, Institute for Great Lakes Research, Perrysburg, O.

    Huron Times, Harbor Beach, Mi., Oct. 22, 1897, from bound newspapers in city clerk's office, Municipal Building, Harbor Beach, Mich.

    Master data file, *Presto*, Institute for Great Lakes Research, Perrysburg, O.

The *Havana* Disaster

A fearful northwesterner was pounding the Michigan coastline as the ore laden schooner *Havana* approached the harbor of St. Joseph at about 10:00 PM the night of October 3, 1887. Rather than risk having his ship dashed against the harbor's breakwater, Capt. John Curran chose to drop anchor a few miles offshore and ride out the storm on the open waters of Lake Michigan. Curran, a Chicago resident and veteran Great Lakes sailor, knew only too well the dangers of attempting to bring a ship through the narrow gates to any port of call in the midst of a gale. Ships that tried it often ended up as broken heaps of wood and metal after they were slammed by the waves against the concrete and rock walls that protected the harbor. His decision to drop anchor and wait out the gale brought moans from the crew, who would have preferred to sleep in a dry and steady bed. The skipper was confident, however, that the *Havana* was a good tight ship and that it could take any pounding Lake Michigan might dish out that night.

Within an hour the storm increased its assault. The wind blew harder and at midnight, the *Havana* found itself rolling and tossing in mountain-high seas, amidst a severe rainstorm mixed with lightning and ear-splitting clasps of thunder. Nobody slept. Curran and all six members of his crew were dressed and hanging on for their lives as the seas rolled over the deck with such weight that it seemed at any moment the ship would founder. One powerful sea swept away the ship's forescuttle, leaving a hole for the water to rush unabated into the hold.

The bilge pumps were started. All night long the men took turns, pumping at thirty-minute intervals. The work on the open deck was so hard and so dangerous the sailors were quickly exhausted. By the end of their half-hour turn they could hardly stand. They pumped all night but the water gained. All they succeeded in doing was keep the *Havana* afloat until dawn. By 8:30 AM Curran knew he had to take drastic action. He told his men to abandon the pumps and, instead, hoist whatever sail they could find. He was going to make a run for shore.

Meanwhile, the citizens of St. Joseph were aware that a sailing ship was in trouble just outside the harbor. The two-master was spotted at about 6:00 AM "standing well off to sea and flying signals of distress," reported the *Daily Palladium* in nearby Benton Harbor. The newspaper said the local life savers were notified, but the seas were so terrible nobody dared to launch a boat and attempt a rescue. Capt. Charles Mulhagen began loading coal in his tug, *Hannah Sullivan,* but it was going to take time before his vessel would be ready. The tug had been stripped for repair and didn't even have water in the boiler that morning. As the word spread around the community, people began lining the lake bank, about six miles north of St. Joseph, where the schooner was located.

Hundreds of people were watching when the *Havana's* sails went up and the foundering vessel started its last-ditch trip toward the shore. A writer for the *Chicago Inter Ocean* described the dramatic events: "The water at this time was within three feet of the hatch combing, and she was sinking rapidly. With all haste her anchor was shipped, and the *Havana* started for the shore under three jibs, the fore and aft sails having been carried away during the night. Laboriously she moved toward the shore, but when within a mile and a half of it, she made a plunge, rebounded, and was about to ride the next oncoming swell when a sea struck her broadside, washed over her, and the next moment she sank out of view."

Capt. W. L. Stevens, keeper of the life saving station, said the moment the *Havana* started its run toward shore, he no longer wanted to wait for the tug. He said he ordered the beach apparatus dragged to the shore. A team of citizens dragged the cannon and breeches buoy equipment five miles until they reached the bluff looking down over the wreck. "We went. . . until we came to the bluff where we could first see the wrecked schooner, which was about one mile in the lake sunk in about forty feet of water," Stevens said. He said the main mast was gone and he could not tell if there was anybody in the ship's rigging. "We left the beach apparatus and ran ahead to find out whether the crew had come ashore or not. When nearly opposite the wreck, we could distinguish objects in the rigging. I hired three rigs to bring myself and the crew to town on the run for the life boat. We reached town twenty minutes too late. The tug *Sullivan* had left for the wreck before we arrived."

Four men could be seen clinging to the crosstrees of the lone mast. They were there for about three hours until the tug battled its way against the storm to reach them. A writer for the *Daily Palladium* said it was a perilous trip for Captain Mulhagen and the six volunteers who accompanied him. "The tug almost stood upon her beam ends as she rounded the north pier and took a nearly straight course for the place where the vessel was last seen. For a half hour the little tug battled with the waves, looking like a smoky speck as it was sighted by hundreds of eyes from along the shore." At last the tug arrived at the wreck, a small boat was lowered and allowed to drift at the end of a rope from the tug up against the wreck. One-by-one, the sailors were helped down from the ropes and into the boat and finally pulled to safety. Survivors were the mate, Samuel McClimen, and sailors Charles Hager, George Shields and R. H. McCormick.

It was learned that when the ship sank, Captain Curran, sailor Joseph Clint and the cook, Joseph Morse, were scrambling up the rigging on the main mast when the mast broke off. All three men fell overboard and were drowned. Clint struck his head against the ship's rail as he fell and was believed to have been killed in the fall. McClimen was badly injured but the type of injury he received was unclear. One newspaper story said his nose was broken and his face badly gashed when he was struck by something. Another story said his arms were broken.

The *Havana* was a fore and aft rigged schooner measuring one hundred and thirty-five feet in length. It was built in 1871 in Oswego, New York. The ship was carrying iron ore from Escanaba, Michigan when it wrecked.

Sources:
    Chicago Inter Ocean, "Found Watery Graves," Oct. 4, 1887, from news clipping file, Institute for Great Lakes Research, Perrysburg, O.
    Daily Palladium, Benton Harbor, Mich., "Wrecked," Oct. 3, 1887, "Three Lives Lost," Oct. 4, 1887, and "Capt. Stevens' Report," Oct. 6, 1887, microfilm rolls, State Library of Michigan, Lansing, Mich.
    Master file containing information about the *Havana*, Institute for Great Lakes Research, Perrysburg, O.

Sole Survivor

Sailor A. J. Slater of St. Joseph was out of his head and talking incoherently when life savers carried him ashore near South Haven, Michigan, on the morning of October 3, 1887. Slater was the only one of the seven-member crew of the schooner *City of Green Bay* still alive after the ship was wrecked in the same gale that sank the *Havana* a few miles away. Like the *Havana,* the *City of Green Bay,* under the command of Capt. P. W. Costello of Chicago, was carrying iron ore from Escanaba, Michigan, to St. Joseph when it got caught in the storm and was driven ashore a few miles short of its destination. The schooner was in trouble and taking on water by the time it hit the beach two miles south of the town at about 8:00 AM. The *Chicago Inter Ocean* said: "When she struck she was waterlogged. She lay exposed here but a short time, the sea coming over her in such violence as soon to break her up, and she fell apart with seven souls aboard."

After his recovery, Slater told his story. He said that once the ship began breaking up, he decided his only chance for survival was to swim to shore. He said he climbed down from the rigging, where he and his fellow crew members had gone after the schooner struck, grabbed a piece of the deck, and used it to buoy himself as he made his perilous swim. The sea almost claimed him. The life savers picked him up about half way to shore. Slater said the other men refused to follow him down from the rigging. They were counting on being rescued there and considered Slater's decision to "swim for it" an act of suicide. They were still there when the ship went to pieces. One-by-one they dropped in the violent sea and were seen no more. The life savers were on their way, but they arrived too late. Killed were Captain Costello, Lars Nelson of Chicago, Henry Booket of Sweden, John Williams of Detroit, Thomas Hoitman of St. Joseph and Patrick O'Leary of Milwaukee.

The *City of Green Bay* had a colorful history that included years of salt water service. The schooner, launched at Green Bay, Wisconsin in 1872, was only two years old when C. W. Elphiche, a Chicago businessman, purchased it, then had it rebuilt and enlarged. After that, Elphiche sent the ship abroad. It sailed down the St. Lawrence River to Quebec, took on a cargo for Dundee, Scotland, then made its first Atlantic crossing in 1877. The ship remained on the Atlantic until the spring of 1880, traveling to such places as Buenos Ayres, Uruguay, Rio Janeiro, Trinidad and then back to Liverpool. It was almost lost in a gale off the coast of Spain, but was picked up by a passing ship and towed to Lisbon, Portugal for repair.

Sources:

    Chicago Inter Ocean, "Only One Saved," Oct. 4, 1887, from newspaper clipping, Institute for Great Lakes Research, Perrysburg, O.

    Daily Palladium, Benton Harbor, Mich., "City *of Green Bay* Lost," Oct. 3, 1887, "The *City of Green Bay,*" Oct. 6, 1887, microfilm rolls, State Library of Michigan, Lansing, Mich.

    Marquette Daily Mining Journal, Marquette, Mich., "The Schooner *City of Green Bay* Goes Ashore at South Haven Yesterday," Oct. 4, 1887, from newspaper clipping file, Institute for Great Lakes Research, Perrysburg, O.

Marquette's Hero: Albert Ocha

    The winter blizzard that swept Lake Superior on Sunday, October 23, 1887 was so terrible that it left many ships wrecked. Among them were the schooners *Alva Bradley* and *George Sherman,* whose pilots both steered blindly that afternoon into the side of Shot Point, about ten miles east of Marquette. The two vessels came ashore so close to each other that the captains could see each other's wreck in spite of the storm.

    The *Sherman's* master, Capt. Nelson Gifford, said he had been following the *Bradley* when the storm first caught the westbound schooners off Whitefish Point, but that he lost sight of the other vessel after the storm intensified and the blinding snow developed. He said the snow fell so thick that it was impossible to see more than a boat's length ahead of the ship. The wind blew first from the northwest, then shifted to the north, sometimes sending gusts of more than forty-miles-an-hour. Tacking against a storm like that required the best seamanship the masters of both vessels could deliver. In spite of their skills, the gale blew the two schooners into the

Michigan shore. Gifford said he knew the *Sherman* was heading into Shot Point even before he could see the land because he could hear the roar of the breakers. "We tried to head off but we were driven hard up on the rocky beach. When I saw that all was up we got the yawl ready and started for shore." The ship began breaking up even as the crew of six men and one woman pulled away in the small boat. The ship's main mast toppled, a portion of the crossbeam striking the yawl, but nobody was hurt. The boat capsized in the breakers and the sailors were forced to swim and wade through the surf to shore. Captain Gifford struck his head against a rock and was temporarily knocked unconscious. Two of the crew members dragged him ashore where he was revived.

The sailors from the *Sherman* stumbled ashore at about 3:30 PM. They were soaked to the skin, suffering from exposure, and badly in need of warm shelter. To their dismay they found themselves in a desolate area. Captain Gifford said he could see the *Alva Bradley* ashore not far away. "She appeared to be resting easy. She struck head on and I thought the crew escaped as she is only a little distance from shore and her small boat was gone. We were in such a fix that we did not stop to hunt anyone else up, as we were lost ourselves." Gifford and his crew, consisting of George Burtis, Ed Lawson, Frank Handy, Dan West, Dave Searles and Kitty Cole, wandered through the snow in the woods for another three hours before they came to a railroad track and started following it. By that time, Cole had become so weak from exhaustion that the men fixed a litter and were taking turns carrying her. After a while a train came along and it gave them a ride into Marquette.

Meanwhile, the crew of the *Bradley* was not safely ashore. The *Bradley's* life boat had been carried away by the storm and even as Captain Gifford was making his cursory examination of the wreck, the ten sailors were frantically tearing away wooden fenders, spars and other parts of the ship to build an emergency raft. They said they were watching the storm tear the *George Sherman* apart and worried that a similar fate awaited them. The sailors spent Sunday night on the wreck and were encouraged when, on Monday morning, four men appeared on the beach. A large bonfire was started as a signal that their plight was known. The storm was still raging, however. Those four men, identified as A. J. Freeman, L. M. Spencer, Robert Gordon and James McConnell, remained on the beach, keeping the fire going, for about another sixteen hours before the rescue was made.

Enter Capt. Albert Ocha, director of the Marquette life savers in 1887. Ocha, described as a daring young man credited with already saving more than twenty lives during his term of life saving service, arrived on the scene a little after midnight Tuesday morning aboard the steam tug *A. C. Adams,* which had a surfboat in tow. With the tug anchored about a mile off shore, Ocha and his crew of eight other men bravely boarded the pitching boat and set off into the darkness, heading for the stranded schooner. Ocha's plan was to pull his craft up on the lee side of the *Bradley,* take off the crew, then row back out to the tug and in this way, escape the terror of going ashore through a killer surf. It was a good idea, but the master of the *Adams* misunderstood his instructions. When Ocha returned to deep water with his prize, the tug was gone.

Ocha was so angry that his first impulse was to order his crew to row an estimated ten or twelve miles through the gale to Marquette. He said he had visions of embarrassing the tug's captain by pulling up alongside the *Adams,* which by then would be safely moored in the harbor, and putting the crew of the *Bradley* aboard. The captain of the *Bradley,* however, objected to the scheme. He said his men were too tired, too cold and too weak to endure such an adventure. Ocha understood and turned the surf boat around, taking them ashore at Shot Point. There they met Freeman, Spencer, Gordon and McConnell at the bonfire. There was food and warmth but little else. The sailors still found themselves in the wilderness. Like the crew of the *Sherman,* everybody trudged through the snow to the railroad tracks and stopped the first train that came along for a ride into Marquette.

Ocha and his crew remained behind because they had the surf boat to salvage. They camped throughout the night until they saw the tug *Adams* returning to its station in the morning. Then they took the boat out to meet it. It was so cold that by the time they reached the tug, the surfmen found themselves frozen to the seat of the boat. Their clothes were coated with ice. When Ocha confronted the skipper of the tug, it was learned that the captain had misunderstood Ocha's direction. As the surf boat was pulling away into the gale, Ocha had yelled "stand by until daybreak." The tug captain said he thought Ocha said "return at daybreak." He just followed orders, he explained.

Source:
   Marquette Daily Mining Journal, "Not a Man Lost," and "A Daring Rescue," Oct. 24 and Oct. 26, 1887, news clippings, Institute for Great Lakes Research, Perrysburg, O.

Wreck of the *E. Cohen*

   There are conflicting stories about just how the schooner-barge *E. Cohen* met its end during a severe storm somewhere off Point aux Barques, Michigan, on October 19, 1890. The *Cohen* and a second barge, the *Journeyman,* were under tow behind the steamer *Eighth Ohio.* All three were carrying lumber from the Saginaw River and bound for Toledo, Ohio. The steamer also was carrying about one hundred and fifty barrels of plaster on the decks.

   As the boats plodded their way from Saginaw Bay and into Lake Huron that Saturday afternoon, they were confronted by a storm out of the northeast that soon put all three vessels in peril. As night fell, the *Eighth Ohio* found itself losing its battle. Great seas, churned by the winds, constantly buried the steamer as it fought to clear the tip of Michigan's little peninsula at Point aux Barques. With the two heavy barges in tow, the *Eighth Ohio* didn't have the power to make headway against the force of the gale. As wave after wave thundered over the decks, the steamer began shipping water. The wooden hatch covers were weakened by the storm and water was pouring into the holds from various places. The captain worried that his vessel would founder. He ordered the crew to jettison the barrels of plaster, and told his wheelsman to steer southeast, keeping the steamer close to the coast. He had thoughts of ducking behind the protective

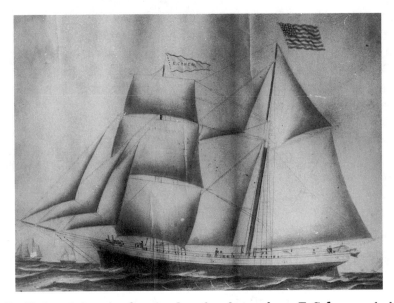

*Conflicting stories exist about just how the schooner-barge **E. Cohen** wrecked near Point aux Barques on Lake Huron in 1890. Courtesy Institute for Great Lakes Research.*

breakwaters at Sand Beach. Somehow the two barges got separated from the *Eighth Ohio*. The tow lines either were cut or they broke in the storm. In the end, the *Eighth Ohio* and the *Journeyman* made it safely to Sand Beach, but the *Cohen* drifted ashore near Port Hope and broke up.

There are two stories. News clips from the *Huron Times,* published at Sand Beach, and the *Democrat,* at Bad Axe, Michigan, said the *Cohen* didn't have canvas for sails and was helplessly adrift until winds blew the ship into the coastal rocks. The stories suggested that the tow line broke. A report in the *Detroit Free Press* and copied by the *Port Huron Daily Times* said the *Eighth Ohio's* skipper cut the tow lines to both barges. The stories said the two vessels set sail, but the *Cohen* didn't clear the coast. There also is a conflicting story about just where the *Cohen* came ashore. Some say it wrecked on Port Hope Reef, due north of Port Hope, while others say it went aground at Burnt Cabin Point, off Grindstone City, a few miles to the west.

Help did not arrive until the next morning, after the *Eighth Ohio* reached Sand Beach, reported the loss of the

Cohen, and a message was dispatched to the Pointe aux Barques lifesaving station. By the time the life savers reached the wreck, there wasn't much left of it. The storm had washed away the cabin and the stern was broken away. Their names are forgotten, but the crew of the *Cohen;* five men and a woman cook, were rescued alive.

In its twenty-three years the *Cohen* appeared on the lakes as first a brig, later a two-masted schooner, and finally a lowly lumber barge. The ship was built at Lorain, Ohio, in 1867.

Sources:

    Detroit Free Press, Oct. 21, 1890, microfilm rolls, Detroit Public Library, Detroit, Mich.

    Huron Times, Harbor Beach, Mich., Oct. 24, 1890, from bound newspapers filed in city clerk's office, Harbor Beach, Mich.

    Port Huron Daily Times, Oct. 21, 1890, from microfilm rolls, St. Clair County Public Library, Port Huron, Mich.

Danforth and *Hayes*

The steamer *A. P. Wright* was no more than two hours away from the safety of Chicago's harbor, with the corn laden schooners *L. P. Danforth* and *R. B. Hayes* in tow, when a storm pounced upon them. The date was April 19, 1893, and the vessels were beginning what was to have been their first trip of the season through the lakes to Buffalo. The gale packed powerful northerly winds and high seas. It was all the steamer could do to hold its own against the tempest.

Troubles developed at about midnight for both schooners. The *Hayes* unshipped its rudder and the crew sent signals, letting the steamer know what happened. At about the same time, the tow line to the *Danforth* parted, sending the schooner drifting off in the night before the gale. The northeasterly winds blew the ship back toward Chicago. By the next morning, the *Danforth* was driven ashore at the foot of Melrose Street, about four miles north of the mouth of the Chicago River. Captain E. L. Hate had distress signals hoisted. Shore watchers were quick to relay the news to the area life savers. Men could be seen hanging in the rigging. The hull was already broken and it was obvious from the way the three master was taking the seas that it was in danger of breaking up. The Evanston life saving crew was the first to try a rescue. While an estimated three hundred people gathered to watch the drama, the life savers launched a boat from the shore and bravely rowed against the powerful surf. Before they got to the wreck, the surfboat capsized. After a few frantic minutes in the water, all of the men stumbled back on shore. They were alive but shaken. Word was telegraphed to Chicago, where another life saving crew was summoned. The second crew decided to use a tugboat to reach the stricken wreck. By the time the tug fought its way to the side of the *Danforth*, the schooner's cabins were torn away and the ship was falling apart. Captain Hate and six other members of his crew were removed safely.

Hate's story of the gale was not well received by the anxious families of the sailors aboard the *Wright* and *Hayes*. He told about seeing the signals of distress hoisted on the *Hayes* and he said he thought this ship also was lost. His prediction was proven correct when the *Wright* steamed back to Chicago two days later without the schooner in tow. The crew of the *Hayes* was safely aboard the steamer, however! The sailors said they abandoned the *Hayes* about thirty miles northeast of Chicago. While they didn't see it sink, the captain said he was sure the vessel foundered within two hours after they left it. The next afternoon the steamer *Atlanta* passed the wreck still afloat about forty-five miles north of Chicago and fifteen miles from Kenosha, Wisconsin. The captain of the *Atlanta* said the peak of the schooner's foresail was set and the vessel seemed to be riding the seas easily. He said he didn't realize that the *Hayes* was abandoned or he would have taken it in tow. The tug *T. T. Morford* steamed out to recover the wayward vessel, but the schooner could not be found. The *Hayes* is believed to have sunk somewhere off Kenosha.

Source:
  Detroit Free Press, "The *Danforth* In Pieces," Apr. 21, and "The *Hayes* Abandoned," Apr. 22, 1893, microfilm rolls, State Library of Michigan, Lansing, Mi.
  Detroit Tribune, "Wreck of the *L. P. Danforth*," April 21, 1893, microfilm rolls, State Library of Michigan, Lansing, Mi.

Spectacular Show At Chicago

Thousands gathered in the rain and wind at Chicago's waterfront on May 18, 1894, because something spectacular was going on just offshore. In spite of the biting wind and rain that chilled the watchers to their bones, few people could tear themselves away from the show. A killer storm was busy wrecking eight schooners and threatening the lives of their crews. People cheered over and over again as local life savers, tug boat captains and civic volunteers got involved in one dramatic rescue after another, sometimes saving sailors against seemingly impossible odds.

Not everybody was saved. All six crew members on the schooner *Myrtle* perished after the ship collided with schooners *Evening Star* and *Gifford,* and then sank. The *Myrtle* was "waterlogged", an old term that identified a wooden ship as flooded and partly sunk, when it tried to drop anchor off the city's breakwater. The watchers gasped in disbelief as the anchor dragged and the half-submerged vessel first slammed into the side of the *Star,* anchored nearby, then drifted off to drive its bow into the side of the *Gifford.* Next the *Myrtle* drifted south before the wind, sinking deeper and deeper as it went. At first the crew could be seen huddling together on the roof of the ship's cabin. Then, one-by-one, the sailors disappeared as waves swept the wreck and carried them overboard. Two men were still clinging to the schooner's rail moments before it sank. Meanwhile the *Star,* which was driven from its anchorage by the crash, drifted against the breakwater where the storm ground it to pieces. Life savers rescued the crew. Three men died trying to escape from other ships as they wrecked in the gale, all within sight of Chicago. But for the efforts of the life savers, the death toll could have been much worse.

The trouble started when the *Jack Thompson* tried to enter the harbor without waiting for a tug, went out of control and collided with the anchored schooner *Rainbow.* The *Thompson* then drifted south, its bowsprit smashed and the foremast gone. The anchor was dropped and for a time it held. As the gale hammered the ship, however, the anchor began to drag and the *Thompson* went ashore, broadside on. Life-savers shot a lifeline across the deck and used a breeches buoy to bring the crew ashore. The ship's cook, Charles Cautlers, drowned when he lost his grip and fell into the sea.

The *Rainbow* also was wrecked. The crew threw out the anchors and tried to ride out the storm outside the break-water. By 3:00 PM this schooner also was drifting south along the coast. The life savers loaded the lifeline apparatus on a flat car of the Illinois Central Railroad, which had track running along the shore. The cannon was fired from various points as the life savers tried to get a line to the drifting wreck, but they couldn't hit the moving target. Meanwhile the tug *Spencer* got close enough to get a line on the *Rainbow's* deck and took off four of the seven sailors before the line broke. The schooner by then was so close to the breakers the *Spencer* pulled away for fear of going on the rocks too. From shore, William H. Havill, a young electrical engineer, tied a rope around his waist and swam about eighty feet to the wreck pulling a small raft. Havill succeeded in getting Capt. John Pew on the raft and people from shore pulled them both to safety. Pew was admitted to a local hospital in serious condition. Havill made a second trip and brought sailor Jacob Kundson to shore the same way. Then E. J. Willis swam out with the raft to save the last man. The other wrecks:

—The *J. Loomis McLaren* broke away from a towing tug and went ashore where it broke up. First Mate Joseph Spolan was killed when the tow line snapped and whipped back on him. The rest of the crew was rescued by life savers before the ship went to pieces.

—The *Mercury* drove before the storm straight on the rocks. Three crew members jumped overboard and nearly drowned before life savers pulled them to safety. A line then was attached and everybody else got ashore by clinging to the rope. The line broke as the last man, Ed Sterling, was half-way to shore. People cheered as volunteers jumped into the water and pulled him to safety.

—The *C. G. Mixer* was arriving with a cargo of railroad ties. The schooner was blown past the harbor where it hit the rocks just south of the harbor. All seven crew members were safely removed.

*The **Evening Star,** left, was one of eight schooners wrecked in a raging gale at Chicago on May 18, 1894. Eleven sailors died in the melee. Courtesy Institute for Great Lakes Research.*

There was one more wreck. The *Lincoln Dall* was driven on the rocks at Glencoe, eighteen miles north of Chicago. Seaman Anton Gunderson drowned trying to swim to land. The rest of the crew clung to the wreck until life savers from nearby Evanston got them safely ashore.

Sources:
    Bay City Times-Press, "Eight Schooners Torn to Pieces by the Fury of the Waves at Chicago," May 19, and "The Wrecks at Chicago," May 20, 1894, microfilm rolls, State Library of Michigan, Lansing, Mich.
    Detroit Free Press, "Disasters! Eight Vessels Driven Ashore Within Chicago City Limits," May 19, 1894, news clipping file, Institute for Great Lakes Research, Perrysburg, O.
    Fond du Lac Daily Reporter, "Death and Havoc Wrought on Lake Michigan," May 19, 1894, news clippings, Institute for Great Lakes Research.

Wreck of the *M. J. Cummings*

The schooner *M. J. Cummings* was caught in the middle of the same storm that played havoc at Chicago. It was early in the day on May 18, 1894, and the crew, under the command of Capt. John McCullough of Marine City, Michigan, met the dawn with great hope of delivery after a long, wearing night on Lake Michigan. Sleep was impossible. The sailors were tired and hungry as the ship approached the harbor at Milwaukee, Wisconsin, driven on by northerly winds.

Captain McCullough was an experienced skipper and he knew bringing his ship safely between the breakwaters would be difficult, if not foolhardy. As desperately as he wanted to find shelter for the ship and to give his worn crew some badly needed rest, he knew that the best thing to do was to drop anchor and try to ride out the storm about a mile off-shore. The masts of another schooner, the *C. C. Barnes,* also were in sight. The *Barnes* also was trying to wait out the blow. The hooks were dropped, but they couldn't hold against the power of the gale. Both schooners dragged their anchors south-ward, past the breakwaters and toward Jones Island. The sailors on the *Barnes* got lucky. Their ship struck soft sand and the crew waited out the gale until they could get safely to shore. The *Cummings,* however, broke its keel when it slammed down on a large boulder. After that the wooden ship began breaking up. The crew scrambled into the ropes to escape the violent seas.

The Milwaukee life savers were watching the drama, and a surfboat was prepared for launching. The nine-member crew pushed off while a gathering crowd watched from the shore. It was live drama happening before their eyes. The life savers slowly worked their way through the dangerous surf, skillfully keeping their frail craft upright. When at last the boat drew alongside the wreck, surfman Frank Goordes, raised himself up over the rail. Almost at the moment that he stepped to the deck of the *Cummings,* the surfboat was struck by a giant roller and capsized. The force of the wave sent the boat flying end-over-end, throwing the other surfmen flying helter-skelter in the foaming seas. By some miracle, all of the men made it back to shore alive, although two were hurt and the boat was so badly damaged that a second attempt could not be made. Word was sent to the Racine life saving station. There a fresh crew arranged to have a special train bring them and another boat to Milwaukee. They arrived late in the afternoon. Meanwhile the storm continued its frenzy with no signs of letting up. After hearing the story of the near disaster by members of the Milwaukee surfmen, the Racine crew decided to try a rescue from a different direction.

By now an estimated six thousand people lined the shores of Jones Island and the nearby mainland to watch the rescue. The surfmen left the harbor in a scow, under tow behind the harbor tug *Knight Templar.* Behind the scow was the empty surf boat. It was nearly dusk when the tug reached a critical spot upwind of the wreck. With its bow to the waves, the *Knight Templar* doled out rope to allow the scow to drop down toward the wreck. Behind the scow, the surf boat drifted closer and closer to the side of the *Cummings.* When the boat was within a few yards of the wreck, a groan went up from the crowd as a human figure, identified as Captain McCullough, slipped from the mizzen mast and disappeared in the broiling seas. He was not the first to die. Thomas Tuscott of Marine City, Michigan, fell to his death earlier in the day. He was followed by first mate Timothy Bosour of Buffalo, New York, and a fourth man, possibly James Whitley, also of Marine City. If any of the remaining sailors were going to come out of this alive, the desperate attempt by the life savers to reach them had to succeed.

At last the empty surf boat was alongside the wreck. It was now up to the stranded sailors to save themselves by somehow climbing down from the rigging and getting into the boat. The people watched as two figures slowly descended the shrouds of the mizzenmast and hung from the ropes only a few feet above the seas. Long minutes passed as the surfmen, working from the deck of the rolling scow, swung the life boat around so that it drifted wildly under the waiting sailors. Everybody knew they couldn't hang on much longer. Their muscles were tired and their hands were numb from the cold. A cry went up from the crowd as the first figure dropped. He landed squarely in the boat. The second man dropped, and also made a successful landing. They were surfman Goordes and sailor Robert Paterson of Kingston, Ontario. Once they were in the boat, it was allowed to drift to shore where they were met by the waiting crowd. Left behind on the wreck, either too weak to save themselves or perhaps already dead were the cook and a fifth seaman, both unidentified. All-in-all, six members of the seven-member crew perished.

The bodies of the woman and man who died in the rigging continued to hang there for yet another day before the storm abated. One reporter said the macabre scene made the bodies appear as "human scarecrows" to the people on shore.

Sources:
    Detroit Tribune, "Six Lost at Milwaukee," May 19, 1894, microfilm rolls, State Library of Michigan, Lansing, Mich.
    Port Huron Daily Times, "Wreck of the *M. J. Cummins* at Milwaukee," May 19, 1894, microfilm rolls, State Library of Michigan, Lansing, Mich.
    Sunday News-Tribune, Detroit, Mich., "Like Human Scarecrows," May 20, 1894, microfilm rolls, State Library of Michigan, Lansing, Mich.

The Tragedy of the *William Shupe*

While the schooner *William Shupe* was not the only ship to meet a tragic end on Lake Huron's rock strewn coast, the story remains more deeply etched in local lore because of the tragic circumstances linked with the wreck. Four Port Huron rescuers drowned on May 19, 1894, when their small boat capsized while trying to reach the *Shupe's* stranded crew near Lakeport, Michigan. The *Shupe* was a typical lake schooner at the turn of the century. The ship had been on the lakes for thirty-two years, which was a long time for a wooden vessel of that period. In spite of its age, Capt. Nelson Little of Port Huron apparently thought the schooner was seaworthy. He invested everything he had to buy the *Shupe* that spring and hired a crew of local sailors. The ship was making its first trip under Little's command from Alpena with a load of lumber. All went well from the time the *Shupe* weighed anchor on May 17 until the next morning when the wind shifted to the north and turned into a gale. When off White Rock, Little said the schooner broached and waterlogged when it was struck from the stern by a monster wave.

"I think it must have been a tidal wave," he said. "I have sailed since I was thirteen and I've never seen anything like it before." Little said he crew had just finished breakfast and he was walking the deck, making sure that the ship was still weathering the storm. "I had just walked forward and turned to come back when I saw her buried in a huge sea. It (the wave) was far above the deck load. The men jumped into the rigging to keep from being washed overboard. The boat broached to the sea taking the forecastle scuttle off, and she filled from there before the water left the deck." The ship was stripped bare by the force of the wave. "We lost all of our head sails in the wind trying to get the *Shupe* out of the trough of the sea, but all in vain. We drifted in that condition until we struck the beach two miles south of Lakeport at 10:00 PM. We were without fire or shelter all that time, constantly wet by the seas that washed over us, with nothing to eat from Friday morning until Saturday night except two water soaked loaves of bread."

The first news of the disaster reached Port Huron on the steamer *Topeka*. The crew of that ship said they passed the *Shupe* in a waterlogged and drifting condition near Lexington, but could not help because of the storm. They said sailors were seen hanging in the rigging. The response was immediate. Capt. A. A. Cox set out on a rescue mission in his tug *C. D. Thompson*. Aboard the tug were John Little, the captain's nephew, Dan Lynn, Barney Mills, Angus King and William Lewis, who volunteered to help. In spite of the storm, the *Thompson* steamed north until it found the *Shupe*. By then the ill-fated schooner was aground. Because of the high seas and the danger of wrecking the tug, Cox was unable to draw close to the wreck. Instead, he launched a yawl with the five volunteers aboard. They reached the *Schupe*, swung their craft carefully around to the lee side, and were securing a line when another giant wave caught the boat. It capsized, dumping all five men in the churning seas. John Little, Barney

131

Mills, Angus King and William Lewis disappeared almost immediately, never to be seen again. Lynn, who was a powerful swimmer, struck out for shore, which was about a thousand feet away. Watchers from shore said Lynn battled against the seas for a long time. He would make some progress but would get caught in an undertow that pulled him back again. Finally, two local men, R. J. "Chubb" Randall and Charles Conkey, attached ropes to their waists, swam out from shore, and with the help of volunteers at the other end of their ropes, pulled Lynn to safety. He was unconscious when they reached him but still alive.

When word of the disaster reached Harbor Beach, about thirty miles to the north, the Pere Marquette Railroad dispatched a special train to speed the lifesavers to the scene. The *Thompson* was still standing by and it assisted in towing the surf boat against the storm to the wreck. This time the rescue was successful. In addition to Captain Little, the rescued crew members included first mate William Brown, James Blair, Reddy Curry and Mrs. Johnson, the cook. A fifth crew member was never identified. The rescuers said Mrs. Johnson fell to her knees and offered a prayer of thanksgiving when she stepped on shore.

The bodies of the four lost men were never found. The families asked Flora Oulette, a Marine City clairvoyant, to help with the search. About a week after the disaster, she walked along the beach, accompanied by several hundred people, but could give no clues. She declared that the bodies were all at the bottom of the lake.

Sources:
   Detroit Free Press, May 19, 20 and 21, 1894, news clipping, Institute for Great Lakes Research, Perrysburg, O.
   Duluth Commonwealth, May 19, 1894, news clipping, Institute for Great Lakes Research, Perrysburg, O.
   Duluth Evening Herald, May 19, 1894, news clipping, Institute for Great Lakes Research, Perrysburg, O.
   Port Huron Daily Times, May 21 and June 2, 1894, microfilm rolls, St. Clair County Public Library, Port Huron, Mich.
   Ruelle, Rick, The life and Death of the Schooner *William Shupe,* 1862-1894, research paper, history file, St. Clair County Public Library, Port Huron, Mich.

*The schooners **Moonlight**, foreground, and **Henry A. Kent** were left high and dry when a storm blew them ashore near Marquette in 1895. Courtesy Institute for Great Lakes Research.*

Left High and Dry

Disaster surrounded them, but the schooners, *Moonlight* and *Henry A. Kent* came out of the incident intact. For a time, however, their fate was in question.

The trouble began the morning of September 29, 1895, when the schooners were under tow on Lake Superior behind the steamer *Charles J. Kershaw*. An early winter gale developed and the three vessels were running for shelter at Marquette. With the harbor almost in sight, a main steam pipe burst in the *Kershaw's* engine room. The steamer lost power and all three vessels drifted at the mercy of the gale until they hit the beach east of the Chocolay River. The *Kershaw* struck a rocky reef and broke its back. As the ship's wooden hull was breaking apart, the crew worried that the wreck might slide off the reef and sink in deep water. The thirteen sailors chose to leave the *Kershaw*. The life boat was launched on the lee side of the wreck. There the sailors stayed, sheltering themselves from the gale as best they could, until the Marquette life savers reached them.

The two schooners came to a stop in the mud where they were walled in by shifting beach sand. When the storm was over, both vessels sat upright, intact, but both were high and dry. People could walk up to the ships and touch their hulls without getting their feet wet. First attempts at salvage were unsuccessful. Before the schooners could be freed, the sand had to be dug away and channels made through which the vessels could be floated back into deep water. The earth that held the ships refused to let them go. The sand refilled a trench as quickly as machines could dig it. One salvager described the situation as hopeless because he said they were dealing with quick sand.

Capt. Byron B. Inman, a prominent Duluth tugboat owner and wrecker, was asked to help. He brought the tug *Record* and five other vessels from his fleet to Marquette on November 1, and a new attempt to dig a trench was made. After a day or two, Inman agreed that conventional methods of digging a trench would not work to free the *Moonlight* and *Kent*. He brought in a special pump used for sucking sand, and attached a long hose. By pumping the sand away from the trench and depositing it in deep water, he found that a channel could be successfully cut. Within days he had the *Moonlight* refloated. Before winter set in, the *Kent* also was free. The story ends tragically, however. One of Inman's salvage tugs used in the operation, the *P. B. Campbell,* foundered on its return to Duluth on December 27. Its complement of seven sailors was lost.

The *Kent* lasted only two years after the mishap. It foundered in another Lake Superior gale in 1897, although the crew escaped. The *Moonlight* sank in a storm, also on Lake Superior, in September, 1903.

Sources:
Beers, J. H. and Co., Chicago,, History of the Great Lakes Illustrated, biography of Capt. Byron B. Inman, Vol. I, p. 44, and data on the loss of the *Kent,* Vol. II, p. 845.
Duluth News Tribune, "The *Moonlight* and *Kent* Stranded on the Beach Near Marquette," Dec. 1, 1895, news clippings, Institute for Great Lakes Research, Perrysburg, O.
Greenwood, John O., "Schooner-Barge *Moonlight*," Namesakes 1900-1909, Freshwater Press, Cleveland, P. 164.
Stonehouse, Frederick, "The Wreck of the *Charles J. Kershaw*," from "The Great Wrecks of the Great Lake," Harboridge Press, Marquette, Mich., 1973, pp. 9-10.

*The tired old lumber schooner-barge **Amaranth** broke in two after it struck the beach at the southern end of Lake Huron in 1901. Courtesy Institute for Great Lakes Research.*

Beached Like Whales

Smoke from a Canadian forest fire mixed with an old-fashioned nor'easter created havoc among vessels caught at the southern end of Lake Huron the night of Sept. 7, 1901. When it was over, eleven ships of all sizes and descriptions were left beached like wayward whales from Harbor Beach south to Port Huron. Two schooners, the *Amaranth* and *John Wesley* broke up and were declared total wrecks. All of the other vessels were later refloated. Local life savers worked through the night removing stranded people from their wrecked and beached ships. A total of fifty-six sailors were brought ashore. Still others chose to remain with their vessels.

People came from miles to see the spectacular sight at Kewahdin Beach, where six ships went aground in one place. They included the lumber hooker *John H. Pauly* and her consort, the schooner barge *Amaranth*, the steamer *Wawatam* and its consort, the whaleback barge *No. 202*, the schooner *Marion W. Page* and the tug *Sarnia*. The *Page* had been under tow behind the steamer *Quito*. The *Quito* also went on the rocks, but then worked its way back into deep water under its own power. The *Sarnia* got hung up while trying to assist the other stranded ships.

Farther north could be found the schooners *John Wesley* and *Vienna*, both aground south of Harbor Beach, the schooner *Andrew Jackson*, the steamer *W. H. Gilbert* and its unidentified consort. The *Wesley* drifted on the beach after it capsized. The ship was carrying lumber from Cheboygan to Buffalo and got caught in the blow off Saginaw Bay. After battling the wind and seas for several hours, the *Wesley's* deck load shifted causing the vessel to list. The crew worked against the storm, throwing the lumber overboard and trying to get the ship back on even keel. By the time the deck load was jettisoned, however, the *Wesley* was waterlogged. Eventually it capsized, going over on its side. The crew was taken off by the Point aux Barques life savers who found the sailors clinging to the wreck about ten miles offshore. The wreck drifted ashore near Harbor Beach.

*Artist's concept of the schooner **John Wesley** under full sail. The **Wesley** capsized and wrecked near Harbor Beach during a storm on Lake Huron. Courtesy Milwaukee Public Library.*

At the south end of the lake, the *Pauly* and schooner *Amaranth* were the first ships to hit the beach. The *Amaranth* broached as it drifted in and immediately broke in two. The skipper of the *Wawatam* saw the lights of the *Pauly* and followed it into the rocks, even though the crew of the stranded *Pauly* shouted warnings. Their voices were overpowered by the roar of the gale. The sailors all said they were blinded by the smoke while battling the storm as they tried to find their way to the mouth of the St. Clair River.

Some of the superstitious crew members on the *Amaranth* had predicted the wreck of their ship. One unidentified sailor later said he saw rats abandoning the thirty-seven-year-old barge as it was taking on its final cargo of lumber at Middleton. The captain said a canary landed on his shoulder, which he believed was a sure sign of impending disaster. The crew of seven survived the wreck, although the ship's cargo of lath boards was left strewn for miles along the beach.

The storm helped convince Congress that something needed to be done to prevent further mishaps. The event led to a decision to anchor the lightship *Huron* as a beacon to ships, leading them into the mouth of the river.

Sources:

Detroit Free Press, stories about the storm, Sept. 8 and 9, 1901, microfilm file, State Library of Michigan, Lansing, Mich.

Duluth Evening Herald, Sept. 9, 1901, news clippings, Institute for Great Lakes Research, Perrysburg, O.

Fond du Lac Daily Reporter, Fon du Lac, Wis., news clippings, Institute for Great Lakes Research, Perrysburg, O.

Port Huron Daily Times, Sept. 9, 1901, microfilm rolls, State Library of Michigan, Lansing, Mich.

Vermillion News, Vermillion, O., Sept. 12, 1901, news clippings, Institute for Great Lakes Research, Perrysburg, O.

The Deep Six

Some people say as many as six thousand wrecks lie at the bottom of the Great Lakes. That may be an exaggeration, although nobody knows for sure. The lore of the lakes includes many stories about vessels that "sailed through the crack." They left port and were never seen again.

*The schooner **New Dominion** created a mystery when it sank on Lake Erie in 1884. The crew was lost. Drawing courtesy Institute for Great Lakes Research.*

Mystery Masts

When the tops of two masts were found eight miles off Lake Erie's Gull Island in late October, 1884, the discovery set off wide-spread speculation as to the ship's identity. The mystery expanded when the body of an unidentified woman drifted ashore at Port Maitland, Ontario, in an unmarked life boat on October 27.

Many believed the vessel was the schooner *Lucinda Van Valkenburg*, carrying coal from Buffalo, New York, to Milwaukee. The *Van Valkenburg* ran into rough weather and laid over at Port Colborne, Ontario, until Sunday, October 26. Its whereabouts were still unknown by the time authorities made lists of potential casualties four days later. Nobody could prove or disprove the *Van Valkenburg* theory. It was not until November 1 that the truth was known. The lost ship was the schooner *New Dominion,* which foundered with a load of coal on route from Cleveland, Ohio, to St. Catherines, Ontario. Lost with this ship were all four members of the crew.

141

Killed were Captain James Griffith, master; Captain John J. Daley, first mate; Daniel Murray and a woman identified only as the captain's sister-in-law, who served as the cook.

Griffith and Daley were both experienced ship's masters who gave up their commands that season to invest in the *New Dominion*. It was an overwhelming debt and to make ends meet, the captains agreed to make the staffing of the ship as much a family affair as possible. Deck hand Murray was probably the only crew member receiving a wage. Now the season was fast drawing to a close and the men were anxious to secure as much freight money as possible. It was said that the *New Dominion* was grossly overloaded and offered little freeboard against the seas when it set sail from Cleveland for its final trip. It was a dangerous thing to have done, but Griffith and Daley were apparently willing to gamble their lives against the few extra dollars they might earn by the time the shipping season ended that winter.

The gamble failed. Nobody knows the horrors these four people endured when the ship encountered rough weather. That the life boat drifted ashore with the cook's body still in it proved that the crew had time to launch the boat before the ship foundered. It was theorized that the others drowned when the boat capsized or else swamped in the surf as it came ashore near Port Maitland. The bodies of Griffith and Murray washed ashore the next day. Among the wreckage was the captain's broken desk, filled with the ship's letters and papers.

Sources:

Beers, J. H., & Co., Chicago, *History of the Great Lakes Illustrated*, Vol. 1, 1899, p 742.

Cleveland Herald, "A Mystery of the Lake," Oct. 31; "Marine Record," Nov. 1; "Wrecked and Missing, Nov. 2; "The Missing Schooner *Van Valkenberg* (sic) Turns Up at Detroit," Nov. 4; "The Lost Schooner *New Dominion*," Nov. 12, 1884, news clippings, Institute for Great Lakes Research, Perrysburg, O.

Collapsed "Like an Egg Shell!"

That was how a reporter for the *Buffalo Evening News* described the sudden destruction of the wooden schooner-barge *Theodore Perry* during a storm on Lake Erie on the night of July 22, 1887. The thirty-two-year-old vessel had apparently become so dilapidated from dry rot and years of neglect that it fell apart under the feet of the sailors who served its decks. Five of the seven people aboard the *Perry* went down with the ship.

The survivors were a Captain McCormack and the mate, Hugh Deering. Both men clung to pieces of wreckage until they were rescued by the steamer *Alaska* about ten hours later. Deering said the piece of the wooden deck that he was riding like a raft was breaking up and he was partly submerged. He said he had resigned himself to death when the crew of the *Alaska* plucked him from the water. He was wrapped in a blanket, which he had grabbed moments before the *Perry* sank. The dead were listed as sailors James Covert of Buffalo, Ben Kennient of Saginaw, Michigan, a female cook identified only as Mrs. Wismenter, and two passengers, Charles Copley of Saginaw, the stepson of the *Perry's* owner, and his friend, Neil McLean, also of Saginaw.

The *Perry* was loaded with coal when it left Buffalo, bound for Saginaw, in tow with three other schooners behind the steamer *D. W. Powers* the night of July 21. The other ships in the tow were the *B. B. Buckhout*, *Senator Blood* and *Wyandotte*. The *Perry* was in second to last place with the *Wyandotte* on the end of the tow line. The vessels got caught in a storm after passing Long Point. The winds swept down from the north, creating cross seas that put the west-bound boats in a constant trough and caused them to strain against their tow lines. Shortly before midnight, when off Rond Eau, Captain McCormack said he sensed that the *Perry* was not responding to its helm and he went forward to make an inspection. He was horrified to discover that the ship was breaking apart. "She was opening up on the starboard side forward just under the deck beams."

Even as he yelled to the sleeping sailors in the cabins below, McCormack said he could feel the vessel breaking up under his feet. Everything was happening so fast there wasn't even time to launch the life boat. The captain said everybody got on deck except the cook before the *Perry* disintegrated and sank. When last seen, the crew was huddled near the fan tail, attempting to launch the life boat. McCormack said he ran into the forward cabin in an effort to rescue Mrs. Wismenter. The *Perry* sank before he got to her. McCormack escaped because the cabin washed away from the sinking ship and he was able to swim out from under it. He said he grabbed the woman once, but then lost her and was unable to find her again. To save himself, McCormack climbed up on the roof, riding it like a raft.

Captain Bennett, master of the *Powers,* was sure that there were no survivors. He said that after the accident, the *Wyandotte,* which was at the end of the tow, was left for a while on its own. Bennett said that when the tow line from the *Perry* was pulled aboard the barge *Senator Blood,* sailors were surprised to see it was still attached to the towing post and part of the ship's head gear. The *Powers* pulled the other barges closer to shore where they found shelter under the lee of the land. Bennett then took the steamer back out on the lake to search for survivors of the *Perry* and to pick up the drifting *Wyandotte.* During the search, Bennett said he saw wreckage, including the cabin, but he didn't realize that anyone was on top of it.

Sources:
>*Buffalo Evening News,* Buffalo, N.Y., July 25, 1887, microfilm file, Buffalo Public Library.
>*Detroit Free Press,* Detroit, Mich., July 25, 1887, news clippings, Institute for Great Lakes Research, Perrysburg, O.
>*Chicago Inter Ocean,* Chicago, Ill., July 25, 1887, news clippings, Institute for Great Lakes Research, Perrysburg, O.

Giant five-masted barkentine **David Dows** *with sails unfurled was a most impressive sight in 1881. The ship was the only five-master ever used on the Great Lakes. Courtesy Institute for Great Lakes Research.*

The Five Master *David Dows*

No collection of stories about Great Lakes sailing ships would be complete without including the *David Dows*. The *Dows,* built at Toledo in 1881, was said to have been the only five masted schooner to appear on the lakes. Its measurements, reaching two hundred sixty-five feet, four inches from stem to stern, placed the *Dows* among the largest vessels on the lakes in its day.

While called a schooner, the *Dows* was in reality a barkentine because it was rigged with square sails on the foremast, and carried fore and aft sails on the remaining masts. The masts themselves towered up to one hundred and sixty-five feet, making the ship a most impressive sight. It took the twelve-man crew between four and eight hours to hoist sail, even with the help of a steam donkey engine to raise the sheets. The holds were large and spacious enough to carry record cargoes of up to ninety thousands bushels of grain. Unfortunately, the *David Dows* turned out to be a problem for its owners, the Toledo shipping firm of Carrington and Casey. The ship was too large to navigate the shallow rivers and harbor entrances of its day while carrying a full cargo, and the barkentine sail arrangement proved to be too cumbersome to make the ship easy to navigate through the turning and twisting routes found on the Great Lakes. Within the first few months, the *Dows* accidentally ran down and sank the schooner *Charles K. Nims* on Lake Erie. The crew of the *Nims* escaped unharmed. Shortly after that, the *Dows* collided with the schooner *Richard Mott* on Lake Michigan, resulting in the deaths of four crew members aboard the *Mott*. After the second accident, the *Dows* was declared uncontrollable and dangerous. The ship was stripped of its top masts and from that time on was used as a tow barge.

The *Dows* met its end in this capacity on November 28, 1889. The ship was carrying coal, and was under tow behind the steamer *Aurora*. Also in tow was the schooner-barge *George W. Adams*. The three vessels were caught in a winter gale which forced the *Aurora* to cut the barges loose off Chicago and then steam into the harbor. Both the *Dows* and *Adams* dropped anchor and prepared to ride out the storm.

The *Dows* did not survive. The ship sprang a leak and its donkey steam engine, which also worked the pumps, failed. The crew was hanging in the rigging when rescued by the tug *Chicago* that night. When tugs arrived at its side the next morning, the *Dows* was sunk to its decks and in danger of foundering at any moment. Attempts to attach a tow line and bring the vessel to safety were hampered by a heavy buildup of ice. Suddenly, even as salvagers watched, the *Dows* reared on its beam ends, dipped its bow into the seas, and disappeared. It sank in forty-two feet of water. When the vessel struck bottom, it righted again, and all five masts reappeared, marking the spot where the big ship went down. It still lies ten miles south southeast of Chicago, partly buried in sand.

Sources:

Clary, James, *"David Dows,"* from Ladies of the Lakes, Two Peninsula Press, Lansing, 1981, pp. 85-95.

Detroit Free Press, "The *David Dows* Founders Near Chicago, Nov. 30, 1889, news clipping, Institute for Great Lakes Research, Perrysburg, O.

Duluth Daily Tribune, "Foundered on the Lake," Nov. 30, 1889, from news clipping, Institute for Great Lakes Research, Perrysburg, O.

Van Der Linden, Rev. Peter, *"David Dows,"* from Great Lakes Ships We Remember II, Marine Historical Society of Detroit, Freshwater Press, Inc., Cleveland, 1984, pp. 95-96.

Dropping Into Self-Destruction

When ships sank in deep water they frequently exploded from air pressure compressed below deck. Survivors often told of violent blasts from the deep after the sinkings. The wooden hatch covers from steel ships almost always separated, indicating an explosive force at work as the ship dropped into deeper and deeper levels. Wrecks of wooden ships seemed to fare even worse. Few of them found on the bottom of the Great Lakes today are intact. The cabins are almost always missing, the decks are usually broken away, and sometimes it is difficult for divers to realize they are looking at the remains of a ship.

The fact that wooden schooners blew up after sinking was dramatically recorded when the schooner *Thornton* sank off Cockburn Island, at the northern end of Lake Huron on August 26, 1870. The *Thornton* was laden with iron ore when it sprang a leak. Captain Lamphere said the crew worked frantically at the bilge pump for about two hours, trying to keep ahead of the water. They even jettisoned the deck load, hoping to lighten the ship enough to make a difference. In spite of their work the water in the hold gained and the *Thornton* settled deeper and deeper. It became obvious that the schooner would sink.

The lifeboat was launched and the crew had just enough time to collect personal belongings and abandon ship. Lamphere said the *Thornton* went down bow first in about three hundred feet of water. As the bow lifted for the final plunge, the heavy cargo of ore shifted to the stern with a loud noise. The shift in weight caused the ship to spear its way with great speed toward the bottom of Lake Huron. There was no time for the compressed air trapped inside the hull and cabins to adjust to the increasing pressure of the water on the outside of the vessel. Within minutes after the ship sank, the water around the lifeboat was disturbed by a violent underwater explosion. Lamphere said pieces of the ship began to surface all around them. The mainmast shot out of the water like a lance, flying completely into the air before falling back into the sea. Then parts of the shattered wooden deck bubbled up. The destruction was so complete, Lamphere said that part of the keel even floated to the surface. The crew landed their boat on Drummond Island, camped there for the night, and then took the life boat on to Detour, Michigan the next day.

∼∽∼∽∼∽

The schooner *Frank W. Wheeler*, exploded in a similar way when it sank in Lake Superior on October 1, 1885. Like the *Thornton*, the *Wheeler* also was carrying a heavy cargo of iron ore, which helped carry the sinking ship rapidly toward the bottom through deep water. The *Wheeler*, commanded by its owner, Capt. William Forbes, was only one year old when it left Two Harbors, Minnesota, on its final trip under tow behind the steam barge *Kittie M. Forbes*. Capt. Daniel Buie, master of the *Forbes*, said the two vessels got into trouble when a northeast gale developed off Keweenaw Point. Both ships were rolling and pitching against heavy seas when the tow line parted. The crew of the *Forbes* spent several hours connecting a new line to the drifting schooner before getting under way again. Two hours later, at about 9:00 AM, Captain Forbes signaled Buie that the *Wheeler* had sprung a leak. Buie said he steered southwest for the shelter of Grand Island. The island was the closest place to go and the new course served to put the wind at the stern of the *Wheeler*. To give the *Wheeler* every chance, Buie also sent some of his crew to the leaking schooner to help man the hand-operated pumps. He said they made the trip at great personal risk in an open boat, rowing against rolling seas.

No matter what the crews did that morning, the *Wheeler* seemed destined to sink. Even though the sailors pumped vigorously, the water gained. The ship pulled harder and harder and eventually was sunk up to its decks. When about eight miles off Point Sauble light, the weight of the waterlogged schooner caused the tow line to break once more. It was then that Captain Forbes lost all hope of saving his command. He gave the order to abandon ship. Fifteen minutes later the *Wheeler* sank bow first. Three separate explosions were heard after it disappeared. The main mast shot up, followed by hundreds of broken pieces of the ship. Buie said he sounded the spot but couldn't learn the depth. The sounding line stopped at fifty fathoms and never hit bottom.

Sources:

Cleveland Leader, "Down in Deep Water," and "Further Account of the Lost Wheeler," Oct. 2 and 5, news clipping file, Institute for Great Lakes Research, Perrysburg, O.

Daily Mining Journal, Marquette, Mich., "Forty Fathoms Down," Oct. 3, 1885, microfilm file, State Library of Michigan, Lansing, Mich.

Detroit Free Press, "Foundered off Sauble Light," Oct. 2, 1885, microfilm file, State Library of Michigan, Lansing, Mich.

Identical stories about the loss of the Thornton, Detroit Advisor and Tribune, Detroit Daily Post and Detroit Free Press, all on Aug. 30, 1870, microfilm file, State Library of Michigan, Lansing, Mich.

Death Ship

The two-hundred-foot long schooner-barge *Comrade* spent its entire seven-year career tethered behind the Gilchrist Steamship Company's steam barge *Columbia*. The two ships appeared inseparable from 1883 to 1890 as they plied the lakes carrying iron ore from Ashland to Cleveland. The companion-ship ended tragically when the *Comrade's* link to the steamer broke in a Lake Superior storm and the ore laden schooner foundered on September 13, 1890, taking its crew of eight sailors to their death.

The crew of the *Columbia*, who did not see the schooner sink, searched the area for the next twenty-four hours, then moored for another two days at Marquette, Michigan, hoping that the *Comrade* would turn up. Thoughts were that Captain Peterson and his crew hoisted sail and used the westerly wind to drive the schooner to a safe shelter, possibly at Isle Royale or else to the lee of Keweenaw Point. The first proof of disaster turned up when the steamship *Winslow* passed through wreckage about twenty-five miles west of Keweenaw. Crew members said they saw fragments of fore and after cabins, railings, spars and other items that marked the wreckage as coming from a schooner. The *Comrade* had originally been built to be a steamer but it never had an engine installed. Consequently, it's silhouette was unique because it was one of the only schooners on the lakes with both fore and after cabins.

The fate of the *Comrade* was confirmed on September 15 when the steamer *John Oades* arrived at Duluth with the schooner's yawl. Captain J. T. Hutton said the overturned life boat was found near floating wreckage in the same area. The discovery of the yawl was a clue that the crew tried to escape their sinking ship. Could it have been that the sailors got away, but then were drowned when the boat capsized? A rope with a plank attached to one end had been tied to the stern of the yawl to be used as a drag, which should have helped the boat keep its head turned into the seas. No bodies were found, which suggests that the vessel sank quickly and the crew lacked enough time to put on life jackets.

The Gilchrist Company came under fire when it was learned that the schooner, which was rated at only nine hundred ten tons, was grossly overloaded with sixteen hundred tons of ore. The *Duluth Evening Herald* on September 19 quoted one unidentified lakes master of saying the ship had been a floating coffin because it was overloaded. He said it lacked adequate freeboard to help withstand the storm.

Sources:

Detroit Free Press, "The Schooner *Comrade,*" Sept. 16, 1890, microfilm rolls, State Library of Michigan, Lansing, Mi.

Duluth Evening Herald, "No Trace of a Vessel," "Floating Coffins on the Lakes," and "The Loss of the *Comrade,*" Sept. 15 and 19, 1890, news clips, Institute for Great Lakes Research, Perrysburg, O.

Duluth Times, "The *Comrade* Gone," Sept. 16, 1890, news clipping, Institute for Great Lakes Research, Perrysburg, O.

Wreck of the *Atlanta*

A late winter storm caught the steam barge *S. S. Wilhelm* and its coal-laden consorts, the schooners *Atlanta* and *Nirvana* on Lake Superior on Sunday night, May 3, 1891. The storm developed into a full-fledged blizzard, complete with blinding snow and freezing temperatures. Wind and waves buffeted the three vessels for hours, and the spray froze to the ships on contact, making it impossible for the sailors to work safely on deck. Conditions deteriorated steadily and by 10:00 PM, the *Wilhelm's* master, Capt. H. Bennett, had enough. He gave the order to turn around and run for shelter behind Whitefish Point, about seventy-five miles to the southeast. The three vessels stayed together most of the night, battling the storm in the best way they could. Then at about 2:00 AM the tow line to the *Atlanta* separated and the schooner dropped off behind the others. Capt. J. L. Knowlton had sails set and the vessel continued to follow for a while. Bennett said he could see the lights from the *Atlanta* off the *Wilhelm's* stern for the next hour. At about 3:00 AM the schooner broached in the heavy seas. "From that moment she never was out of the trough." Bennett said he thought the *Atlanta's* crew couldn't manage the ship anymore because of the heavy buildup of ice on the deck, sails and rigging. "It was next to impossible to do anything with the canvas, as the water froze on everything it touched."

The *Atlanta* continued to drift for several hours. The ship's new hull remained water tight for a while, in spite of the pounding it took. Once a vessel broaches, the waves assume a broadside assault, taking their most destructive shots. Wooden hulled ships were not built to take that kind of punishment. By the time the sun was up, the schooner was taking on water. Knowlton estimated that it was just a matter of time before the *Atlanta* would sink. At about 11:00 AM, he gave the order to abandon ship. Captain Knowlton and the six members of his crew spent the next seven hours battling the storm in an open boat rowing an estimated twenty miles toward shore. They approached near the Number Ten life-saving station, where life savers were on the alert to possible trouble. A lookout saw the little boat before it attempted to land, and a crew was preparing to go out to meet them when disaster struck. The yawl capsized in the breakers, drowning all but two of the seven tired and struggling sailors. Both survivors were in such a bad condition the next day they could not be interviewed. They were identified as John Pinto and Eli Waite.

Sources:

    Detroit Free Press, "The *Atlanta* and Five Men Lost," May 7, 1891, microfilm rolls, State Library of Michigan, Lansing, Mich.

    Duluth Daily News, "Wreck of the *Atlanta*," May 6, 1891, news clippings, Institute for Great Lakes Research, Perrysburg, O.

    Duluth Evening Herald, "The Story of Capt. Bennett, Who Towed the Wrecked *Atlanta*," May 11, 1891, news clippings, Institute for Great Lakes Research, Perrysburg, O.

    Marquette Daily Mining Journal, "Schooner Believed to Have Been Lost in Monday's Gale," May 6, 1891, from microfilm rolls, State Library of Michigan, Lansing, Mich.

Sinking Fast On Lake Michigan

The schooner *Mediterranean* was an old ship when it dropped unexpectedly to the bottom of Lake Michigan during rough weather on September 25, 1891. Built at Sodus, New York in 1859, the vessel had been plying the lakes for thirty-two years, which was a relatively long time for any wooden-hulled ship. Its owner, Capt. E. G. Kohnert, expressed surprise after the ship sprang a leak and sank so quickly off Sheboygan, Wisconsin. Crew members escaped with only the clothes they were wearing. Kohnert said he thought the *Mediterranean* was in good condition and he had no idea why it foundered. "I spent two thousand, five hundred dollars in rebuilding her last winter," he said.

The ship left Alabaster, on Saginaw Bay, early that week with a load of rock plaster bound for South Chicago. The lake was whipped with a brisk southwest wind on Friday and the seas were running high. Kohnert said all was going well until about 9:00 AM when the wheelsman complained that the ship wasn't answering its helm. It was discovered

*Schooner **Mediterranean**, at right, sank so quickly on Lake Michigan the crew barely had time to get away. Courtesy Institute for Great Lakes Research.*

that the hold was flooded and that the *Mediterranean* was sinking. There was no time to start the pumps. The crew ran to the stern where the sailors grabbed life preservers and launched the yawl. They had only pulled about two hundred feet away before the ship capsized and sank.

Captain Kohnert said that even though the lake was rough, the day was warm and the crew didn't suffer. Even at that, everybody was glad when the sails of an approaching ship were spotted about an hour later. The vessel turned out to be the schooner *John Mee*, which stopped and took them aboard. "It was a welcome sight," Kohnert said. "There was rejoicing in our lifeboat."

Source:
    Chicago Inter Ocean, "The *Mediterranean* Founders in a Heavy Sea," Sept. 28, 1891, news clipping file, Institute for Great Lakes Research, Perrysburg, O.

"Like a Load of Lead"

The life savers at Milwaukee station jumped into action the blustery morning of September 30, 1896, when the steam barge *B. W. Arnold* appeared off shore with a foundering schooner in tow. Even as they pulled on their weather clothes and launched the surf boat, the men knew that they could not waste a moment. The schooner *Sumatra* was already sunk to its decks in heavy seas and someone in the *Arnold's* pilot house was leaning on the whistle cord. It seemed as if the sailors were crying out about the urgency of their need for help.

The task of rescuing the sailors from their sinking ship was going to be a dangerous one. The storm was packing thirty-mile-an-hour winds that were creating seas that looked like mountains to men in an open boat. The crew leader, a man identified only as Captain Boutin, enlisted the help of the harbor tug *H. W. Simpson*. The tug steamed out of the harbor with the surf boat in tow. To save time, the life savers rode in the surf boat. The plan was for the tug to get up wind and then slowly back toward the sinking schooner until the surf boat could be pulled alongside.

Meanwhile, the sailors aboard the *Sumatra* were working desperately to keep their ship afloat until help arrived. Captain Charles Johnson of Bay City, Michigan, said the vessel had been leaking since it left Chicago the night before with a load of railroad iron, bound for Fort William, Ontario. Even with the pumps operating, the water was gaining. As the storm intensified, the seas washed over the schooner's decks, carrying away pieces of the ship one board at a time. Now, at about 2:30 AM, while within sight of Milwaukee, Johnson knew time was running out. The *Sumatra* was sinking. The hatch covers were torn away and every wave now was sending water cascading into the hold. Now the tug *Simpson* and the surf boat it had in tow were in sight. At last, help was on the way.

The end came so quickly that the crew was caught by surprise. "She seemed to go down like a load of lead," Johnson said. "The crew didn't even have time to mount the rigging."

The sinking ship took all seven members of the crew down with it, drowning four. Johnson lived because the *Sumatra's* life boat broke loose and floated away, and he managed to get into it. He was rescued by the life savers who reached the boat only minutes before it drifted to destruction against the Milwaukee breakwater. Also saved were John Burbeck, the mate, and Ira Purser, the cook. Both were pulled aboard tug which found them swimming in the water after the schooner sank.

The tug's engineer, Robert Werley said he had yet another sailor by the hair and was about to pull him on board the *Simpson,* but lost his grip when a large piece of drifting timber struck the man. The body sank before the tug could turn around and make another pass. Killed were Arthur Burnsted, Charles Hemmer, Patrick Peterson and Peter Anderson. All of the crew members were from Bay City.

Source:
  Duluth Evening Herald, "Schooner *Sumatra* Sinks Off Milwaukee Harbor Entry This Morning," Sept. 30, 1896, news clipping, Institute for Great Lakes Research, Perrysburg, O.

Sinking of the *Antelope*

Some ships changed from schooners to barkentines and even to steamers and back again during their years on the lakes. The *Antelope* was such a vessel. It began its existence in 1861 as a steamship carrying passengers and freight. It served in that capacity until struck by fire at Buffalo, New York, on November 16, 1867. After that, the hull was towed to Detroit, Michigan, where it was lengthened and the vessel rebuilt as a two-hundred-foot long barge. In 1888 the *Antelope* was rebuilt again and rigged as a three-masted schooner.

The *Antelope* was still a schooner when its rotting thirty-year-old wooden hull fell apart. It happened while the ship was under tow behind the steamer *Hiram W. Sibley.* The coal-laden schooner foundered on Lake Superior, near Michigan Island of the Apostle Group, on October 7, 1897 when

The schooner **Antelope** *as it appeared before it foundered in Lake Superior in 1897. Photo furnished by Institute for Great Lakes Research.*

about one hundred and thirty miles from its destination at Duluth. The schooner developed a leak early in the day and the crew started working the pump, hoping to keep the ship afloat until it reached Duluth. After several hours, however, the leak got worse. When it was evident that the *Antelope* was going to sink, Captain Allson T. Angres signaled the *Sibley* and the steamer stopped to take the crew of seven sailors aboard. From the deck of the *Sibley* Angres and his crew watched the old ship sink. It lies in about three hundred sixty feet of water.

Owner L. S. Boulett of Bay City refused to talk to reporters about the sinking and he swore the crews of both the *Antelope* and *Sibley* to silence. Details of the incident were absent from all of the news stories that month. Speculation grew, however, (it may have come from a crew member who talked anonymously to a newspaper reporter) that the old *Antelope* broke up under the strain of the rough seas and power of the steamer, which was pulling the *Antelope* along at a speed of about twelve miles an hour. In other words, the schooner was running in fast company that day, and it did her in.

Sources:

    Detroit Free Press, "*Antelope* Founders," Oct. 9, 1897, news clipping, Institute for Great Lakes Research, Perrysburg, O.

    Duluth Evening Herald, "The Schooner *Antelope,* Coal Laden, Founders in Lake Superior Yesterday," Oct. 8, 1897, news clipping, Institute for Great Lakes Research, Perrysburg, O.

    Duluth News-Tribune, "Old Craft Sinks, Oct. 8, and "*Antelope* Loss About $14,000," Oct. 10, 1897, news clipping, Institute for Great Lakes Research, Perrysburg, O.

    Marquette Mining Journal, "*Antelope* Sunk," Oct. 11, 1897, from microfilm file, State Library of Michigan, Lansing, Mich.

"She was a Floating Coffin . . ."

When the board of inquiry convened at Mulford's Undertaking Parlors in Port Huron, Michigan, on Monday, July 24, 1899, sailor Edward Farley was present. It was an angry Farley who appeared to make serious accusations against Captain McDonald and the Detroit owners of the ill-fated schooner *John Breden* lying sunk about fourteen miles north of the city. Port authorities wiped their sweaty brows in the heat of the afternoon, and tried not to stare too much at the bloated body of the ship's cook, Jane Conners, as Farley told his version of the grim facts leading to her death and the deaths of two other sailors.

"She was a floating coffin," Farley said of the *Breden.* He said he was convinced that he was alive to tell his story because he jumped ship at Port Huron, after serving as a member of its crew for the ride north from Toledo. He said "continued hard work at the pumps had been necessary to keep her from sinking." Farley claimed that he personally furnished a row boat when he first shipped on the *Breden* because the schooner didn't have a life boat in its davits. He made the decision to leave the ship because he feared for his safety, and also he hadn't been paid. The last straw came when port authorities seized the vessel for unpaid debts on July 8, the day it arrived at Port Huron. Farley wanted a safer birth. He said it was his opinion that the thirty-seven-year-old schooner was so rotten from age and neglect that when it encountered a storm while under tow behind the tug *Winslow,* "the *Breden* broke up from the strain." He also suggested that the *Breden* was overloaded. With six hundred tons of coal in the hold, the ship far exceeded its gross tonnage allowance recorded at just over three hundred tons.

Capt. McDonald denied the charges. He said he believed the *Breden* was seaworthy and said he never would have weighed anchor if he wasn't convinced of it. He said the ship had bad luck when it ran into a northerly gale that was too much for it. "Everything went all right until we were off Lexington, when the tug turned back. After we turned the pumps were sounded and twelve inches of water found in the hold. I called all hands to the pumps, but while they were pumping I saw that the vessel was about to founder. I called to the cook to come where I could help her, and in less than fifteen minutes the *Breden* had gone to the bottom. The tug turned back and did everything possible to save us. I do not know the names of the men who were lost. They shipped at Port Huron before we left."

The schooner's seams opened up and it sank in forty feet of water, taking Jane Conners and the two others sailors to the bottom with it. McDonald said the other survivor was sailor Joseph Benson. "I have sailed for many years and do not think that the wind was too strong for the barge. Something gave way and she filled in a few minutes," he said.

Sanilac County sheriff's diver Garry Biniecki, who found the wreck in the summer of 1994, said the vessel appears to have fallen apart when it struck the bottom. He said the sides of the *Breden* lie separated from the rest of the vessel. There also is a possibility that the wreck was destroyed with dynamite. A story in the *Port Huron Daily Times* said the vessel sank in forty feet of water directly in the shipping lane and was considered a threat to passing vessels.

Sources:
    Detroit Free Press, July 22, 1899, microfilm rolls, State Library of Michigan, Lansing, Mi.
    Port Huron Daily Times, July 22, 23 and 24, microfilm rolls, State Library of Michigan, Lansing, Mi.

A large crowed turned out for the launching of the four-masted schooner **Minnedosa** *at Kingston, Ontario, on April 26, 1890. The* **Minnedosa** *was the largest sailing ship ever built in Canada. Courtesy Institute for Great Lakes Research.*

One Last Brave Act

The story was told that Capt. John Phillips and his crew died heroically because they took a moment to cut a tow line to a trailing barge as the schooner *Minnedosa* sank under their feet. Survivors said the action saved the schooner *Melrose* and its crew from getting pulled down with the *Minnedosa*.

It was October 20, 1905 when the *Minnedosa* was lost with all hands on Lake Huron, off the tip of Michigan's Thumb District. At the time, Capt. Alex Milligan, master of the steamer *Westmount,* which had both the *Minnedosa* and *Melrose* in tow, said he thought someone used an ax to cut the tow line between the *Minnedosa* and the *Melrose* moments before the four-master foundered in a gale. Diver and lakes historian David Trotter confirmed the story when he discovered the lost schooner in 1993. "The steel tow bit still has three layers of rope wound on it. We could see where someone cut the rope with an ax. The story is true. They cut the *Melrose* free," Trotter said.

Captain Milligan said the three ships fought bad weather from the moment they left Fort William, Ontario, with their holds loaded with wheat bound for Kingston. The storm intensified and turned into a gale while the vessels were crossing Saginaw Bay. The *Minnedosa* by then had sprung a leak and was getting waterlogged, which hindered progress. The three ships were estimated to be moving no more than five miles an hour against the storm. "We were moving in toward the shore. Harbor Beach was but eight miles away and we were getting in toward shelter when the line from the *Minnedosa* to the *Melrose* was cut. I intended to keep on with the *Minnedosa,* realizing she was so battered and laden that she must get out of the storm, and hoped the *Melrose* could keep together until I could get back to her," Milligan said.

He said the *Minnedosa* sank so fast that nobody on the *Westmount* saw it go down. "The mate, John Black, was watching the *Minnedosa.* He said he looked away for a moment, and when he turned back the ship was gone." The deck crew rushed to the stern where they saw the steel towing cable dropping straight down in the lake like an anchor chain. Black said the windlass was turned and the cable came up with a jerk. At the other end of the line was the towing post from the bow of the *Minnedosa.* It had been torn from the wreck.

Captain Phillips had his wife aboard the *Minnedosa* that fateful day. They died together with seven other members of the crew. No bodies were found when Trotter dove the wreck. Trotter, a Ford Motor Co. executive, said he found the schooner using sonar. The discovery was kept a secret for months to give Trotter and other members of their group, Undersea Research Associates, time to examine and photograph the wreck without being disturbed. As he did with the *Hunter Savidge,* a wreck story which appears on page 9, Trotter has kept the exact location of the *Minnedosa* a secret.

The *Minnedosa* lies about two hundred feet down, which would make it a dangerous wreck for sport divers to visit. Trotter's team used special deep diving equipment to reach and photograph it. He said the schooner lies in an upright position. All four masts are broken or toppled, apparently from the collision when the ship struck bottom. The impact caused other structural damage to the deck and the cabins are collapsed. Other than that, the wreck is intact. "We even found the life boat lying next to the ship," said Trotter. "It is really unusual to find a lifeboat still on a wreck."

According to Trotter, the two hundred and forty-three-foot-long ship was the largest schooner ever built in Canada and it was one of the few four-masted sailing ships used on the Great Lakes. He said he believes it is the only four-masted sailing ship lying sunk in Lake Huron. Trotter said he searched for the *Minnedosa* on and off for about fifteen years. "It was always a mystery just where it sank. The captain of the *Westmount* gave a location that was wrong. I think he was confused by the storm and didn't really know where he was."

Sources:
Detroit Free Press, "Fierce Storms Wreck Vessels and Carry Sailors to Death," "*Minnedosa's* Crew Met Death Bravely," and "Her Cargo Swamped Her," Oct. 21, 23 and 25, 1905, news clippings, Institute for Great Lakes Research, Perrysburg, O.
Duluth Evening Herald, "To Save Consort, Crew of the *Minnedosa* Cut Loose and Soon Went Down," Oct. 23, 1905, news clippings, Institute for Great Lakes Research, Perrysburg, O.
Notes from interview with David Trotter, October, 1993.
Port Huron Daily Times, "*Minnedosa* Foundered off Harbor Beach," Oct. 23, 1905, microfilm file, St. Clair Public Library, Port Huron, Mich.

The Tasmania Also Goes Down

The same storm that sank the *Minnedosa* on Lake Huron also sent the four-masted schooner-barge *Tasmania* and eight sailors to the bottom of Lake Erie. It was a tragic end to a ship that had known days of glory when it first slid down the ways at Port Huron thirty-four years earlier. When launched as the *James Couch* in 1871, the two hundred twenty-three foot-long ship was among the first of a new line of super transports, designed to compete in the ore and grain trade following a government deepening and widening of locks and waterways connecting the Great Lakes. The *Couch* was so large that it could only carry partial loads during the first years of operation. The government dredging program wasn't completed in 1871, and a severe draught caused the lake water levels to drop.

By 1905 the schooner had gone through various owners and at least one name change. It was suffering from dry rot and warped timbers, but still actively involved in hauling ore when the end came. It happened during the pre-dawn hours of Friday, October 20 as the storm was buffeting the steamer *Bulgaria* and its two tow barges, *Ashland* and *Tasmania* near Pelee Island. The crew of the *Ashland* said the *Tasmania* was the end barge in the tow. They said they saw the schooner's lights one minute as the ship rode the crest of a mighty wave, but then the vessel dropped in a trough and the lights disappeared. The *Tasmania* was never seen again.

*The **Tasmania** was among the first four masted schooners on the lakes when launched as the **James Couch** in 1871. The vessel sank on Lake Erie in 1905 killing the entire crew. Courtesy Institute for Great Lakes Research.*

It was as if the seams were torn open and the ore-laden vessel dropped like a stone. The crew might have had a few moments warning because there was evidence that someone launched the life boat. A boat from the *Tasmania* was found floating upside down a few days later. No bodies were found. Killed were Capt. William Radford, mate George Whitesell, and sailors Austin Methew, Michael Boyle, August Ulbrick, John Trapp, J. R. Stough and Harry Lapask.

All three vessels were traveling from Escanaba to Cleveland with ore. After the *Tasmania* disappeared, the *Bulgaria* and *Ashland* dropped anchor behind Pelee Island and rode out the storm. The gale that sank the *Tasmania* was one of three major storms that swept the lakes during the fall of 1905. In all, forty-two vessels were damaged, run aground, or sunk. Twenty-one lives were lost.

Sources:

    Detroit Daily Post, "Launch of the *James Couch*," Apr. 25, 1871, microfilm rolls, State Library of Michigan, Lansing, Mich.

    Erie Daily Times, "Eight Drowned" Oct. 24, 1905, microfilm rolls, Erie Public Library, Erie, Pa.

    Greenwood, John O., "Schooner-Barge *Tasmania*," Namesakes 1900-1909, Freshwater Press, Inc., Cleveland, page 104.

The *Checotah* Story

The tired old wooden schooner-barge *Checotah* had already lead a perilous life before it came to its final resting place at the bottom of Lake Huron, twelve miles northeast of Port Sanilac, Michigan, on October 30, 1906. During the early days, when the vessel was known as the schooner *George D. Russell,* it was involved in a collision with the propeller *Northerner* and sank with iron ore in its holds. The accident happened in the St. Marys River, just south of Sault Ste. Marie on September 9, 1882. Three sailors died. The *Russell* was written off as a total loss by insurance companies. Because the wreck was lying in the middle of a busy shipping lane, however, an effort was made to raise it. The tug *Gladiator,* equipped with two divers, steam hoists, tackle and other salvage equipment, succeeded in raising the schooner and bringing it into dry dock for rebuilding. With new timbers and new owners, the ship started its new life in 1890 with a new name, *Checotah*. Despite the changes, bad luck continued to haunt the vessel. The *Checotah* stranded on Thunder Bay Island, in Lake Huron, on May 28, 1899. Tugs again came to its rescue.

The storm of October 30, 1906, spelled the end of the barge. The *Checotah* was carrying lumber, the second of three lumber barges in tow behind the steamer *Tempest,* when it sprung a leak, became waterlogged and threatened to sink. The crew of the *Tempest* cut the tow line and left the foundering barge at the mercy of the storm. In retrospect, it seemed to have been a cruel thing to have done, but attempts by the *Tempest* to save the *Checotah's* crew might have put that ship, plus its other tow barges, the schooners *Uranus,* and *M. McVea,* in jeopardy.

The master of the *Checotah* was Capt. William Somerville of Berlin Heights, Ohio. On the ship with him was his daughter, Kate, first mate William Lee of St. Clair, Michigan, and sailors Robert Carey, William Fray and Peter Wood, all of Port Huron. Somerville gave the order to abandon ship. The sailors were lucky. They spent about an hour in an open boat before they were picked up by the passing steamer *W. A. Payne*. The *Payne* took them on to Port Huron.

The wreck was found by Sanilac County divers in 1988, located about twelve miles northeast of Port Sanilac, Michigan. Garry Biniecki, a county deputy, and teachers Tim Juhl and James and Pat Stayer said the wreck lies in more than one hundred feet of water. They said the *Checotah* is badly broken after sinking bow down and hitting the lake bottom. The wreck rests upright, tilted slightly to starboard. The deck and cabins floated away. The starboard side is peeled back from the hull.

The *Checotah* remained on the lakes from 1870 until its loss in 1906. The ship measured one hundred ninety-eight feet in length.

The schooner **Checotah** *sprang a leak and foundered in Lake Huron in 1906. The crew escaped in the ship's life boat and was picked up an hour later by a passing steamer.*

Sources:

Cleveland Herald, "More About the Late Collision," Sept. 9, 1882, news clipping, Institute for Great Lakes Research, Perrysburg, O.

Diving Times, "The Search for the *Checotah,*" by Garry Biniecki, Spring 1989, page 1.

Duluth Evening Herald, "Family Crew Rescued," Oct. 30, 1906, news clipping, Institute for Great Lakes Research, Perrysburg, O.

Duluth Tribune, "Marine Matters," Oct. 20, 1882, news clipping, Institute for Great Lakes Research, Perrysburg, O.

Port Huron Daily Herald, "*Checotah* Founders," Oct. 30, 1906, microfilm rolls, St. Clair County Library, Port Huron, Mich.

Toledo Blade, "Rescued in the Lake," Oct. 31, 1906, news clipping, Institute for Great Lakes Research, Perrysburg, O.

The Christmas Tree Ship

Rats were part of the lore of sailing ships in the old days. The vile creatures seemed to always be around the ship's galleys where quantities of flour, sugar, lard and other staples used in preparing meals were stored. For some strange reason, sailors included them in their superstitions. The mariners reasoned that rats were good sailors and knew secret things about the future. When rats were seen leaving a ship in port, it was taken as a sign that the ship was going to sink.

That is what happened on the schooner *Rouse Simmons*. As the crew was preparing the ship for a trip across Lake Michigan in November, 1912, sailors noticed rats coming out of the hawser pipe and dropping into the water. The phenomenon bothered sailor Hogan Hoganson enough that he jumped ship when the *Simmons* arrived at Manistique, Michigan, to pick up its annual load of Christmas trees. "All the way across the lake, as we sailed for our cargo, the old saying had been ringing in my head . . . the rats always desert a sinking ship," Hoganson said.

Capt. Charles Nielson, the ship's master, also knew about the rats. Nielson told Capt. George DeMar of the Chicago harbor police that he feared that it was a bad omen. The sixty-eight-year-old Nielson was an experienced sailor who didn't want to make the trip. He told his sister, Mrs. Alvida Verner, that he had a premonition that something was going to happen before he returned. But Nielson said he had promised Herman Schuenemann, the owner of the forty-four-year-old schooner, that he would make the trip. "I know the *Simmons* isn't safe, but I promised to go and I can't go back on my word," he told her.

Hoganson worried about the omen of the rats until the *Simmons* got to Thompson's dock at Manistique, and then he developed a new worry. He said he really made his decision to leave the ship after watching Schuenemann overload the vessel with trees. "When he had filled the hold with Christmas trees, we were ordered to pile up a deck load. The load grew and grew and still they had us piling more and more

*The **Rouse Simmons** arrives in Chicago with its decks laden with Christmas trees. The ship sank in a Lake Michigan storm while bringing another load of trees in 1912. Courtesy Institute for Great Lakes Research.*

trees on top," Hoganson said. "I protested to Captain Nielson, telling him that if we struck heavy weather, the boat would be too top-heavy to weather it. But the captain seemed to think he knew more about it than a seaman, and ordered us to pile more trees on deck."

The *Rouse Simmons* sailed from Manistique, bound for Chicago, on November 21 with Nielson, Schuenemann and nine other sailors aboard. The ship encountered a heavy winter gale and never arrived at Chicago. The *Simmons* might have been seen once before it foundered. A schooner was spotted on Saturday, November 23, off Kewanee, Wisconsin. The vessel was laboring heavily in a maze of snow and rain and was flying distress signals. Local life savers tried to launch a boat but were driven back by the storm.

All hope that the *Rouse Simmons* might turn up faded on December 3 when wreckage, including quantities of Christmas trees, washed ashore at Pentwater, Michigan. The news cast a pall over the holiday season in Chicago, where the arrival of the Christmas tree ship each December was becoming a tradition. Schuenemann docked his ship at the Clark

Street Bridge where he sold his trees for a quarter to a dollar. The wreck was discovered by a diver in 1971 off Two Rivers, Wisconsin. The *Simmons* lies in one hundred eighty-five feet of water. Divers say the hold is still filled with trees.

Sources:
    Chicago *Record-Herald*, stories from Nov. 30, Dec. 3, 5 and 6, 1912, news clips, Institute for Great Lakes Research, Perrysburg, O.
    Duluth Herald, stories from Dec. 3 and 4, 1912, news clips, Institute for Great Lakes Research, Perrysburg, O.
    Greenwood, John O., "Schooner *Rouse Simmons*," from *Namesakes 1910-1919*, Freshwater Press Inc., Cleveland, p. 28
    Master data file, Institute for Great Lakes Research, Perrysburg, O.
    Ratigan, William, "Christmas Trees for Davy Jones," from *Great Lakes Shipwrecks and Survivals*, William B. Eerdmans Publishing Co., 1960, pp. 38-39.
    Toledo Blade, "Ship Carrying Christmas Trees Goes Down in Lake," Dec. 4, 1912, news clips, Institute for Great Lakes Research, Perrysburg, O.

Night Rescue

When the schooner-barge *Santiago* sprang a leak and sank in calm water off Lake Huron's Point aux Barques on the night of September 9, 1918, it provided a spectacular view for the passengers of the passing steamship *City of Alpena*. The passengers lined the rail of the *Alpena,* many of them awestruck as the crew of the *Santiago* scrambled from the listing barge to the deck of the steamer *John F. Morrow*. They later described the rescue as both dramatic and daring. The commander of the Harbor Beach life saving station later said he thought the *Morrow's* skipper, a man named Sullivan, deserved a medal.

The *City of Alpena* stood by for several hours, its searchlight trained on the sinking barge, while the crew of the *Morrow* brought their ship alongside to make the rescue. The light, which cast an eerie glow on the disaster scene, added to the drama of the moment. The *Alpena's* passengers were probably disappointed when they missed seeing the *Santiago* sink. The barge floated for hours, long after the *City of Alpena* steamed on its way. Captain Sullivan had hoped to tow the ill-fated vessel into nearby Harbor Beach, or at least get it to shallow water. There wasn't enough time for that. The

*Schooner-barge **Santiago** under tow at Ashtabula, Ohio. The ship foundered in Lake Huron in 1918. Courtesy Institute for Great Lakes Research.*

Santiago sank in deep water about fourteen miles off shore. Wreckage, including a yawl boat, an oar and other pieces of debris, washed ashore the next day.

The *Santiago* was in tow behind the *Morrow* when the barge got into trouble. Both vessels were downbound with their holds filled with iron ore. The *Santiago* was a large vessel measuring three hundred twenty-four feet in length. While originally designed as a three-masted schooner, the ship spent most of its life between 1899 and 1918 used as a tow barge.

Sources:

Greenwood, John O., "Schooner-barge *Santiago,*" Namesakes 1910-1919, Freshwater Press, Cleveland, Ohio, 1986, page 353.

Master data sheet, Institute for Great Lakes Research, Perrysburg, O.

Port Huron Times Herald, "Boat Goes to Bottom, Crew Saved," Sept. 12, 1918, microfilm rolls, State Library of Michigan, Lansing, Mich.

Big Barge Down

There were many wooden tow-barges operating on the Great Lakes before the turn of the century, but few of them were as impressive as the three hundred and twenty-two-foot-long ore carrier *Chickamauga.* Built at Bay City shipyards in 1898 especially to serve as an ore carrier, the *Chickamauga* was a super ship in its day, with a hull that stretched longer than some of the steamships that pulled it. Few boat watchers could let the barge pass without taking a second look. It was big.

Almost from the day that steam-powered ships began operating on the lakes, owners saw the value in tow-barges. While steamboats were powerful and more dependable than sail-powered ships, they had a disadvantage. A large part of the cargo space had to be filled each trip with coal or wood for fuel. With a tow barge trailing, a steamer had the ability to carry twice and sometimes triple the amount of cargo with every trip. Some ship owners assigned two or three schooners to their steamships. The schooners served as barges. Instead of having its steamers pull a string of small barges, the Mentor Transit Co. of Detroit ordered the *Chickamauga* built .

The *Chickamauga* had a carrying capacity of forty-three hundred gross tons. The ship had three holds, separated by wooden bulkheads, and its hatches were spaced on twenty-four foot centers to accommodate the iron ore chutes at upper lake docks. The barge operated successfully until the fall of 1919, when it sank in a Lake Huron storm near Harbor Beach. It was laden with forty-one hundred tons of ore, under tow behind the steamer *Centurion,* on route from Escanaba to Cleveland, when the two vessels got caught in the storm on Saginaw Bay the afternoon of September 12.

At about 3:00 PM, Capt. Carl Johnson, master of the barge, began blowing a distress signal, letting the *Centurion* know that there was trouble. The barge had sprung a leak and the ship's bilge pumps were not keeping up with the rising water in the hold. The *Centurion's* skipper, Capt. J. L. Bradshaw, couldn't talk to Johnson against the roar of the storm, but he guessed correctly what was happening. His trained eye told him that the big barge was riding too low in the water. He turned the steamer and started a race against time toward the newly built harbor of refuge at Harbor Beach. It was a close race and they almost made it. With less than a half mile to go, the *Chickamauga* sank in about forty feet of water just outside the harbor entrance. The crew of ten men and one woman rode the ship down as they were frantically trying to launch the life boat. As the barge settled, the wooden decks and pilot house broke away. Crew members either jumped or were thrown in the seething water. Everybody was wearing a life jacket. All the sailors were picked up alive by the tug *James Whalen,* operated by Capt. Robert Graham.

Wreckage from the *Chickamauga* still lies on the bottom of the lake just northeast of the breakwater. Divers say it doesn't look much like the old barge. The ship was an obstacle to other vessels so dynamite was used to blow it apart.

Sources:

Greenwood, John, *"Chickamauga,"* Namesakes 1910-1920, P. 326, Freshwater Press, Cleveland, O. 1986.

Master data file, Institute for Great Lakes Research, Perrysburg, O.

Port Huron Times Herald, *"Chickamauga* Founders Near Harbor Beach," Sept. 13, 1919, Microfilm rolls, St. Clair County Library, Port Huron, Mi.

Schooner-barge **Chickamauga** *sank near Harbor Beach during an autumn gale in 1919. Courtesy Institute for Great Lakes Research.*

Narrow Escapes

If sailors have guardian angels the angels were working overtime during the golden era of sailing ships on the lakes. Stories about miraculous rescues were commonplace.

The *Paragon* Horror

Heavy weather caught the tug *William A. Moore* and its tow of five lumber barges on Saginaw Bay. The lumber laden vessels were working their way through Lake Huron on a trip from Saginaw past Detroit to Lake Erie ports. It was October 16, 1868 and the *Moore,* a three-year-old vessel, was towing a fleet of timeworn wooden schooners and scows, drawn from a ragged fleet left on the lakes immediately after the close of the Civil War.

The storm intensified as the line of boats worked easterly around the tip of Michigan's Thumb District and into the open lake. Somewhere off Point aux Barques the trailing barge, the *Hercules*, sprung a leak and waterlogged. Because it was still under tow, the *Hercules* began dragging like a giant sea anchor, slowing down the progress of the other vessels and putting extra strain on the tow lines. The *Moore* forged on around the coast, eventually turning south toward the St. Clair River. The harbor of refuge at Sand Beach was only a dream in 1868, so the *Moore* didn't have the option of taking shelter there. The steamer continued on, each member of the crew hoping the storm would abate and that the barges would make the safety of the river without getting into trouble.

The tow line parted when off Lexington, sending all five barges floating off to battle the storm on their own. The crew of the *Moore* tried to pick up the tow again, but in the attempt, the tug collided with the barge *Paragon* and put a hole in its side. The old boat filled with water and, like the *Hercules,* it waterlogged. It settled so low that the seas were washing the decks and flooding the cabins. There was no dry place on the ship so the crew climbed into the rigging. In addition to Capt. Wilson Searles, the crew included Margaret Darby, her teenage son and ten-year-old daughter. At least four other unidentified men also were hanging in the ropes. Waiting out a Lake Huron storm for hours in the rigging of a partly sunk sailing ship was no easy task for a young, able-bodied seaman. It was torture for Mrs. Darby, a woman of forty years, and her two children. The best one can do to protect the body against the onslaught of the cold wind and spray from the rain and sea is dress warmly. After hours of clinging to the ropes, the arms get tired, hands get so numb one can no longer feel anything at the tips of the fingers, and the pain from the aching muscles becomes overpowering. As the night wore on, the weak ones began to die.

Mrs. Darby's son was the first to go. After hours of silence, he announced that he could no longer hang on. Captain Searles told a haunting story about how young Darby told everybody good-by before he let go. His body dropped away into the raging sea and disappeared. After that, two other men quietly dropped to their death. Searles said Mrs. Darby's daughter died in his arms. Moments later, Mrs. Darby died. He said he and the remaining sailors felt they too would soon be dead. As they waited for what they though was the inevitable, the Canadian gunboat *Prince Alfred* steamed alongside and took them aboard. The *Paragon* was towed to Sarnia, Ontario, where it was declared a total wreck. The crews of the other drifting barges were rescued alive by area tugboats.

Sources:

    Detroit Free Press, "Barge *Paragon* Lost," Oct. 20, 1868, microfilm rolls, Detroit Public Library, Detroit, Mich.

    Toledo Blade, "A Chapter of Disasters, Oct. 20, "Terrible Suffering and Loss of Life on the Lake," Oct. 23, 1868, news clippings, Institute for Great Lakes Research, Perrysburg, O.

*The **Goshawk** rigged as a schooner-barge near the final days. The ship was operating under sail the night it nearly lost its crew in a snowstorm near Chicago. Courtesy Institute for Great Lakes Research.*

Lost Crew of the *Goshawk*

The schooner *Goshawk* had just cleared Chicago harbor and was starting the first trip of the season in the year, 1880, carrying grain north on the first leg of a long trip to Buffalo, New York, when sailor Frederick Cook slipped from the boom of the mizzen mast and fell overboard. The accident on the evening of Tuesday, April 6, couldn't have happened at a worse time. The ship was tacking northward against brisk northwesterly winds, night had just fallen, and there was a heavy snow falling. The ship's mate, James Corcoran, saw Cook tumble. He threw a plank overboard, hoping to give the man something to hang onto until a lifeboat got back to him. He knew it would be a miracle if Cook was recovered alive.

A ship under sail doesn't have any brakes. The best the crew could do was turn the vessel into the wind in such a way that the sails work against the forward motion of the ship. By the time the *Goshawk* was stopped and a boat lowered, it had traveled a long distance from the point where Cook tumbled in the water. Corcoran also knew that the wa-

177

ter in Lake Michigan in April is so cold Cook probably died from hypothermia within a few minutes after he fell. Nevertheless, the mate launched the boat and seamen Henry Crosby, James Lynch and Nelis McTaggard volunteered to help him conduct a search. The *Goshawk* was light handed for the trip, so Capt. Edward Morton, the second mate and the ship's cook were the only ones left on board as the lifeboat disappeared into the dark and whirling snow. Morton and Corcoran shouted to one another to give the men in the lifeboat some sense of direction. After a while they could not hear each other.

The *Goshawk* remained anchored for the rest of the night, but the yawl never returned. The next morning the ship was spotted anchored offshore with distress flags flying, and life savers at Chicago went out to investigate. It was found that the three people left on board couldn't raise the anchor without help. The tug *Annie L. Smith* steamed out of Chicago and brought the schooner back into port. Fears mounted that day for the rest of the *Goshawk's* crew. Captain Morton got the tug's skipper, Captain Eph Wilson, to go back back out on the lake in search for the boat. Hours of searching turned up nothing. It appeared that the *Goshawk* lost five members of its crew only a few miles out of port.

Before nightfall, however, Corcoran and the other three sailors arrived in town on a northbound train. They said they searched in vain for the missing sailor, and then realized that not only was Cook lost to them, but so was the schooner. They battled the seas all night and finally were blown ashore several miles south of Chicago. They walked back toward the harbor until they came to a railroad track and flagged down a passing train.

Source:
    Chicago Inter Ocean, "Experience of the Crew of the *Goshawk*," Apr. 8, 1880, news clippings, Institute for Great Lakes Research, Perrysburg, O.

Aboard the *Ida Belle*

When the crew of the Canadian scow *Ida Belle* came ashore in a life boat near Cleveland, Ohio, shortly before noon on September 7, 1880, the word soon spread that the ship was lost on Lake Erie. That wasn't entirely true. The *Ida Belle* was sunk to her decks about eighteen miles north of Cleveland, but it did not founder. It was a wooden ship filled with cloth and lumber. The harbor tug *L. P. Smith* steamed off that afternoon and returned a few hours later with the wayward scow in tow.

Capt. T. Depew, master of the *Ida Belle,* told his story to the *Cleveland Herald* that evening with all of the flavor of an experienced sailor after years under the mast. His colorful account appeared in the newspaper the following day without editing:

Depew said the scow weighed anchor and sailed from Rondeau, Ontario, at 10:00 PM on September 6 with a cargo of bolts and cord wood. He did not give the ship's destination. From the southeasterly course he chose, it might have been Buffalo. "An hour later the wind began to freshen and the gaff topsails were taken in. The wind was then east northeast, from which quarter it blew nearly all night. The gale increased and there being a beam sea, caused the vessel to surge badly. At midnight it was discovered that she had sprung a leak and had begun to fill. In less than half an hour, two feet of water rose in the hold, making it necessary to work the pumps constantly to keep the vessel afloat. During all this time a tremendous sea broke over the scow, deluging the cabin and making matters decidedly uncomfortable.

"At four o'clock the wind shifted to the northward and the vessel, which had been almost at the mercy of the wind and waves for several hours, sailed steadily toward Cleveland. She made good headway until between nine and ten o'clock in the morning when she broached to with the wind and became unmanageable. The mainsail was removed, leaving the jibs and foresail, but still the scow would not pay off," the story said. Land was visible but from eighteen miles, it was too far away for distress signals to be spotted. It was at this point that Depew and Robert Brigham, the ship's owner who also was on board, gave the order to abandon ship. With the wind and sea at their back, the small boat carried everyone to shore in less than two hours.

When it arrived in port, the *Ida Belle* was badly waterlogged. The deck load of cord wood had been swept away by the seas. The cabins were drenched. The leak was caused when boards on the port side near the bow separated.

Source:
   Cleveland Herald, "The Scow *Ida Belle* Founders in Lake Erie," Sept. 8, 1880, news clipping, Institute for Great Lakes Research, Perrysburg, O.

"She Sprung a Butt!"

Captain Bedford was in such an exhausted state when rescuers hoisted him from his wrecked and waterlogged command that he could not tell his story until the following day. Bedford and the three other members of the crew of the capsized schooner *William R. Hanna* knew only too well that it was their own seamanship and their combined will to survive that had saved them from certain death. After gaining his senses at a private home at Harbor Beach, Bedford granted an interview to a reporter for the *Huron Times.*

He said the *Hanna* was loaded with sixteen hundred heavy tamarack railroad ties, downbound across Lake Huron and heading for Toledo, when it got caught in a winter gale off Saginaw Bay. The date was Friday, November 5, 1880. "We took in our main sail and let her jig along under the foresail and staysail, having blown away our jib. At three-thirty o'clock (in the afternoon) we sighted the Port Austin reef light. We turned east-southeast to clear the reef and immediately ran into heavy seas. She labored heavily but did not take on any water until we got past the point, when she sprung a butt and filled so fast the pump was of no use."

By 6:00 PM the ship was waterlogged and out of control. It was no longer responding to the turn of either rudder or sail. The *Hanna* broached and then capsized in the heavy seas. The mate was at the wheel and one man stood by him. As they felt the ship going over, they jumped for the windward rail but lost their grip and were thrown backward into the water. Captain Bedford said all crew members were on the deck and they found themselves swimming for their lives. It was a most dangerous place to be because by November, the temperature of Lake Huron was low enough to kill. Luckily the ship did not turn completely over but went on its side, with a few feet of the vessel still out of the water. Rope rigging remained in place, leading from the side of the schooner angling downward to the top of the masts. "As quickly as possible we all climbed into the main rigging," Bedford said. "Our feelings at the time, in a raging sea, black darkness surrounding us, snow falling heavily and great waves dashing over us every instant, can better be imagined that described. I confess, for my own part, I had no hope of ever seeing home or friends again."

The four desperate sailors drifted in that state for about three hours. And then something most amazing happened. They saw lights ahead and realized that they were drifting southward toward Harbor Beach. The wreck passed within about five hundred feet of the breakwater. "We shouted at the top of our lungs for help. We saw lights moving here and there on the breakwater and we had every hope that someone would come to our rescue. But as we drifted past the pier and no help came, our hope died."

At about this time the wind shifted from northeast to northwest and Bedford knew that if something wasn't done, the wreck would be blown out into the middle of the lake where almost certain death awaited. Although numb with cold and finding it difficult to move about, Bedford and the others forced their way forward along the rail, using their knives to cut away the weather lanyards. It was a reckless gamble but it worked. As the ropes separated, the *Hanna* slowly returned to an upright position. The men then could make their way to the bow and drop the anchor. They were still close enough to the harbor to be spotted in the morning. It was a long, cold night. The sailors huddled together on the partly submerged deck, using their own body warmth to keep each other alive, while getting deluged by constant seas and pelted by snow and freezing spray. The ship's cabin had been washed away and there was no shelter to be found. They were still there when the steamer *L. Worthington* came out of the harbor the next morning to pick them up. The other crew members were Sylvester Roy, mate, and sailors Ralph Finelson and John Susa.

Source:
> *Huron Times*, Nov. 11, 1880 edition, bound volumes stored at city clerk's office, Harbor Beach, Mich.

*The schooner **Negaunee** is riding deep in the water indicating heavy cargo. The vessel survived a serious storm on Lake Erie in November, 1880. Courtesy Institute for Great Lakes Research.*

The Race to Cleveland

Riding out a November gale on Lake Erie in the schooner *Negaunee*, anchored off Fairport, Ohio, was bad enough, but Captain J. A. Holmes was informed at about 8:00 PM that there were three feet of water in the hold. The bilge pump was started, but an hour later when the water level below deck was raised to four feet, Holmes knew his ship was sinking. The *Negaunee* was loaded with over one thousand tons of coal, bound from Buffalo to Chicago in tow behind the steam barge *Henry Chisholm* when the two vessels got caught in the storm on November 21, 1880. The seas ran so high that the *Chisholm's* engines couldn't fight the storm and pull the *Negaunee* at the same time. The schooner was cut loose to battle the wind and waves on its own. Such was the fate of some schooner barges in tow before the turn of the century. The water was shallow enough that Captain Holmes chose to drop anchor and let the ship's bow turn into the wind. After that, it should have been a matter of waiting until the storm was over.

It would have worked, but for a broken centerboard chain. Sometime during the storm, while the sailors gripped the railings on the deck of the rolling, tossing, ice laden ship, the chain snapped, causing the centerboard to drop free. After that, there was an open spigot of water pouring in. Holmes sent a small boat ashore to get help. The Freeport life savers came but even with the additional manpower taking turns at the hand operated pump, the water gained. Even in the best weather, the sailors couldn't work the pump fast enough to keep ahead of this leak. Word was sent to Cleveland, and the tugs *George N. Brady* and *Forest City* steamed out to the rescue. The *Brady* was the first to arrive alongside the stricken ship. By then the *Negaunee* was low in the water with seven feet of water in the hold. Sailors were not only pumping, but they were tossing the cargo of coal overboard to lighten the ship. The *Brady* brought additional pumps and manpower, and then took the *Negaunee* in tow. By about 5:00 PM the *Forest City* arrived and also put a second tow line on. It was a race against time.

183

The *Negaunee* made it. After arriving in Cleveland harbor at 11:00 PM, the exhausted sailors stopped pumping. Within minutes the ship settled gently to the bottom, where it rested until workers raised it and brought it into dry dock for repair. By then the cabin room doors were warped from the flooding. The davits were bent and the life boat floated away. The damage was extensive, but the crew was saved. The schooner was repaired to sail again. It remained on the lakes another twenty-six years, not meeting its end until stranding in a gale at Lake Erie's Cedar Point in 1906.

Cleveland Herald, "The Schooner *Negaunee* Sunk," Nov. 24, 1880, news clippings, Institute for Great Lakes Research, Perrysburg, O.

Master date sheets, Institute for Great Lakes Research, Perrysburg, O.

Riding a Waterlogged Raft

It was by mere chance that a lookout on the steamer *Wisconsin* thought he heard human voices in the dark waters of Lake Michigan and reported to the wheelhouse. The steamer stopped that cold brisk morning of November 21, 1882 and picked up sailors R. D. Sheldon, Frank McFee and Nicholas Johnson, the only survivors of the schooner *Collingwood* which foundered two days earlier somewhere off Grand Haven, Michigan. The three miraculously stayed alive for twenty-one hours; the final hours standing on a partially submerged piece of the wooden deck. They said the *Collingwood* was carrying a load of cedar pails from St. Helena to Chicago when it sprang a leak in rough weather and foundered.

Johnson told his story to the *Duluth Daily Tribune*: "The gale was blowing from the nor'west and about five o'clock the sea made the vessel roll over," he said. "There we lay, right on broadside, till the topmast went out, when with a great groan she straightened up on her beam-ends and kept that way for about an hour. Then, all of a sudden, the deck burst up, caused by the pressure of the water against the cargo, and she rolled over and went down head first. The whole crew, eight of us, were all hanging for dear life to the taffrail, thinking that it would give way. After she went down the sea washed over us. The captain and the three other men who were lost were seen floating with posts under their arms. There was a piece of deck about six feet square and three of us got on to that. Sheldon got onto another raft, the one we three were on when we were picked up. Four of us finally got onto that raft. We suffered terribly, the air being biting cold, and a fierce gale was blowing. To make matters worse the steward became a raving maniac on Thursday night, and it was all that two of us could do to keep the poor fellow on the raft. All through the night and during Friday the man fought us, and several times succeeded in getting into the water, but we dragged him out. About four o'clock yesterday afternoon his strength gave out and after a last maniacal struggle, he died. We held onto his body awhile, but had to let it wash overboard.

"Early yesterday morning all of us became almost totally blind from the terrible exposure. The raft gradually began lowering as the posts under it absorbed the water, and from dark on until the time we were found we stood in water the whole time nearly knee-deep. We continued walking from one end to the other, and someone would occasionally go to sleep while walking and step overboard. The others would pull the unfortunate back onto the raft. For twenty-one hours we didn't have a thing to eat. I managed to dig a little bit of oakum out of the raft and the three of us chewed this for twelve hours. McFee would have died in a couple of hours if we hadn't been picked up. He was beginning to act crazy and was so numb that it was with difficulty that we kept him on his feet."

News accounts could not agree on the name of the captain. Of the three stories found, the names Milletts, Willis and Willets were given. His age ranged from 45 to 60. The newspapers agreed that the captain lived in Kingston, Ontario.

Sources:
   Detroit Free Press, "The Schooner *Collingwood* Lost in Lake Michigan," Nov. 26, and "The Loss of the *Collingwood,*" Nov. 28, 1882, microfilm rolls, State Library of Michigan, Lansing, Mich.
   Duluth Daily Tribune, "Founders on the Lake," Nov. 28, 1882, news clipping, Institute for Great Lakes Research, Perrysburg, O.

Against Impossible Odds

That all seven members of the wrecked brigantine *William Treat's* crew survived was counted miraculous after they spent six days and nights adrift on storm-tossed Lake Huron without food or shelter. Captain McKay's emaciated frame shocked friends and family when he returned to his home in Bay City, Michigan, on October 11, 1883. When a reporter for a Bay City newspaper came to the house the next day, McKay told a story of terror and suffering that few sailors have ever experienced and lived to talk about. Had the wreck occurred only a few weeks later in the season, when Lake Huron was a few degrees cooler, the story might have been more tragic.

McKay said the *William Treat* and the schooner *Seminole* left Bay City for Detroit, both loaded with lumber and under tow behind the tug *J. P. Clark*, on Thursday, September 27. The *Treat* was the end boat in the tow, following behind the *Seminole*. "When off the Charities in the afternoon the wind freshened, and at nine o'clock that night, when off Sand Beach, the sea was very rough." At about that time, McKay said he noticed lights and activity at the stern of the *Seminole* and suspected that his ship was about to be cut adrift. He said he shouted and asked the *Seminole* "to hang on to his line. The captain of the *Seminole* replied that he had already let go." The tug and *Seminole* then put into Sand Beach for shelter, leaving the *Treat* to fend for itself in the storm.

Before sails could be set, the brig broached against the seas. McKay said it shipped so much water that by midnight the *Treat* was partially sunk and waterlogged. Even with sails set and the crew working the bilge pumps, he said the vessel could not be brought around again. The crew, consisting of mate George Aikens, the cook Annie Livingstone, seamen John McQuee and Oliver Alien and two other men whose names were not given, first climbed on top of the lumber piled on the deck to escape the seas. McKay said everybody watched anxiously for daylight, hoping the *Clark* would come back and get them. There was no tug. No ship was seen that morning or all the next day. The storm rolled off to the east and by noon Friday McKay said the lake got so calm the water looked like glass under the hull of the drifting wreck. With the hull full of water, the vessel was impossible to control. In its half-sunk condition, water splashed over the deck. The cabins were wet and unlivable. The fires in the galley were extinguished by the high water so food could not be prepared. Because the *Treat* was floating somewhere in the middle of Lake Huron, and completely out of sight of land, the crew elected to stay with the ship and wait for a passing vessel to take them off.

No ship came Friday or Saturday. Another storm developed on Saturday night. This gale blew from the northwest and pushed the wreck toward the Canadian shore. McKay said everybody hung on, too tired and exhausted from hunger and exposure to do anything else, as the vessel rolled and tossed under them. During the second storm the ship began breaking up. McKay said a part of the stern tore away and he could see pieces of lumber floating away. By Sunday morning the wreck was within sight of the Canadian shore and the captain thought perhaps, once the wreck grounded, a rescue would be forthcoming. It didn't happen. The fickle lake winds shifted in the afternoon and the *Treat* was blown back into the lake again.

Monday night yet another storm developed. This became a gale of even greater strength than the two previous storms. Again the helpless crew hung on to the rolling, pitching vessel, believing that each assault against the striking seas would be their last. The torture continued for hour after hour. Strangely, after this new menace passed the wreck beneath them was still holding together and they were still alive. McKay decided that no ship was coming and that if they were to survive, the crew of the *William Treat* was going to have to do what it could to rescue itself. He reasoned that the ship was still relatively close to the Canadian coast, even though he could not sight land. The lifeboat had been carried away by the waves so by noon on the fifth day the men were busy building a raft from spare pieces of lumber and rope. "Having no awl nor hatchet we used a pocket-knife to manufacture paddles out of boards. About 3:00 PM the mate, George Aikens, and cook, Annie Livingstone, and two seamen went on board the raft and paddled for shore, distant about eighteen or twenty miles." The three sailors were the stronger among the group. They took the cook so she would have a chance. They were too tired to paddle their raft with any speed and that night another storm swept the lake. The suffering the four sailors endured on that open raft was known only to themselves. Yet there was a positive side. The wind blew the frail craft close to shore and in the morning it struck the beach a few miles from Goderich. The four stumbled ashore, finding it difficult to believe they had been finally delivered from the tempest and that they were still among the living! They came to the farm home of Alexander Young, who took them in and gave them food and shelter. Young was so moved by their story that he immediately traveled to Goderich for help.

In the meantime Captain McKay tried to set some kind of makeshift sail and use the westerly winds to blow the wreck closer to shore. As the storm swept the waterlogged decks, the men stood in water sometimes up to their waist, hoisting sheets to a mast. As the sails put pressure on the mast, the men were dismayed to hear a deep cracking noise. Everybody backed away as the mast collapsed to the deck. He said it fell so hard that the pole broke in three places. Later, when the ship thundered to a stop after striking a reef, it began falling apart. The bow, deck and a portion of the deck load fell away on impact. McKay and sailor John McQuee built another makeshift raft and then let the storm carry it to shore with them on it. They left Oliver Alien behind. Alien refused to get on the raft and said he would take his chances on the wreck. Farmer Young saw the second raft coming in and was on shore to meet it. McKay and McQuee were so weak they said they might have drowned in the surf without Young's help. He brought them ashore and then had them carried to the farmhouse. Alien also made it. He came ashore on a portion of the bow, sharing the wreckage with the captain's dog.

Source:

  Cleveland Herald, "Story of a Miraculous Rescue," Oct. 16, 1883, news clipping, Institute for Great Lakes Research, Perrysburg, O.

Riding into Cleveland on a Breeches Buoy

November 1, 1883 was a cold breezy day but hundreds of people crowded the old Lake Shore Railroad freight pier at Cleveland, Ohio, to watch the drama of shipwreck unfold. It began early in the day, while the gale was whipping Lake Erie into a frothing caldron, and the schooner *Sophia Minch*, heavy with iron ore, sought safe refuge behind the stone breakwaters. The *Minch* dropped anchor outside the harbor and waited for the tug *Patrick Smith* to steam out and tow it safely through the harbor gap. The *Smith* didn't have a strong enough hawser to pull the heavy ship against the storm. The line broke, the *Minch* drifted off and stranded at the mouth of the Cuyahoga River. The hull was scuttled to keep it from pounding, and the Cleveland life savers, under the command of Capt. Charles C. Goodwin, spent the day bringing the crew safely to shore.

That evening, with the shadow of the wrecked M*inch* still in clear sight, the people braced themselves against the brisk biting offshore wind to watch as still another sailing ship, this time the three-masted schooner *John B. Merrill,* approached the harbor. The ore-laden ship came in with all but the foresail reefed. Even with bare masts, the storm whisked the schooner past the piers as two tugboats, the *James Amadeus* and *N. B. Gates*, raced to it's side. The seas were so high the two tugs seemed to the watchers to be bobbing about like corks as one-by-one they disappeared behind a wave, then rose to ride the tip of another. The *Amadeus* reached the *Merrill* first and took a line. Once it was secure, the people watched as black smoke belched from the tugboat's stack as it strained to turn the ship around and get its head into the wind. Luck was not with the sailors that night. About the time the *Merrill* was turned, the tow line parted. By this time the *Gates* was on the scene and together the two tugs worked to secure a new hawser between the *Amadeus* and the *Merrill.* Again the tug steamed hard against the storm, inching the heavy schooner around the breakwater and toward the harbor entrance. People said the *Amadeus* pulled so hard they swore they saw fiery sparks flying from the stack.

Just as it looked as if the *Merrill* was going to be safe, the tow line broke again. The things that happened after that became an almost carbon copy of events earlier in the day. Just like the *Minch*, the *Merrill* drifted off before the wind, heading for the beach. The anchors were dropped, but they found no purchase. Nothing worked. The *Merrill* drifted past the *Minch* and grounded on the rocks about fifty feet away.

Captain Goodwin, who at the age of forty-two had a reputation as one of the most daring and successful life savers on the lakes, decided to use a device called a breeches buoy to rescue the stranded sailors. The breeches buoy employed a pair of short-legged canvass trousers, commonly called breeches, which were attached to a rope on block and tackle connected between the wreck and solid ground a few hundred feet away. Sailors could be carried ashore one-by-one by climbing into the breeches and waiting for someone from shore to pull them in. It was a very effective way of saving people from ships driven close to shore in storms. Because vessels have a deep draft, they rarely got close enough to solid land for the shipwreck victims to save themselves by wading ashore. When it worked, the buoy was considered safer than carrying people ashore through the surf in an open lifeboat. The trick was in getting the hawser line from shore to the

*The **John B. Merrill** was one of three vessels blown ashore during a series of gales at Cleveland in 1883. Courtesy Institute for Great Lakes Research.*

wreck. A common way of sending the line was by cannon. A rope was attached to a special ball that was fired over the deck. The rope, in turn, was attached to the hawser, which was pulled aboard by the sailors on the wreck. Problems sometimes developed when the people on the wreck didn't know how, or were, for one reason or another, unable to hook up the breeches buoy. When this happened, someone from shore had to make a daring trip through the surf in an open boat to reach the wreck and do it for them.

The equipment was set up and the mortar fired at about 7:30 PM. The ball settled down over the wreck in a perfect line on the first shot. There was a lot of shouting back and forth between the wreck and the men on shore as instructions were sent for securing the lines and setting up the breeches buoy. When, at last, it seemed as if things were ready, someone on shore agreed to test the equipment by riding the breeches out to the ship. A life-saver named Hatch volunteered for the job. He climbed aboard the frail appearing little device and held on while ready hands began pulling the ropes that sent him off into the darkness. Everyone knew that if anything went wrong, Hatch could fall to his death in the surf below. Nothing went wrong. Hatch made it to the wreck and a few minutes later his shout: "Haul ashore!" was heard. The people strained their eyes as the life savers pulled on the ropes and the basket reappeared first as a speck in the dark sky. In it was a woman, the captain's wife. The basket was sent back and one-by-one every member of the *Merrill's* crew was delivered safely ashore. Rescued were Captain Jerry Coleman, his wife, first mate Daniel McKenzie, second mate Patrick Coleman, and sailors Patrick McManus, Nicholas Peterson, Manuel Vieira, John Jongeblod, Anton Lorenzen and Daniel Hanley.

A Repeat Performance

Ten days later the schooner *John T. Johnson* was anchored off Cleveland harbor, riding out another offshore November gale, when the anchor dragged. The ship, under the command of Capt. Christy A. Peterson, arrived on the afternoon of November 11, loaded with iron ore, in tow of the steambarge *Ohio*, but then cast off to enter the harbor under sail while the *Ohio* and a second vessel in tow, the *Charles Ryan,* steamed on down the lake toward Fairport. The fate of the *Ryan* in the same gale is told in the following story. The storm developed at about 7:00 PM while the *Johnson* was about twelve miles offshore. By the time the schooner reached the Cleveland harbor and dropped anchor off the east pier lighthouse, the ship was a shambles. Its fore-boom and nearly all of the canvas was carried away. The anchor dragged and soon the schooner was driven aground at the end of the pier.

The local life savers saw what was happening. They lost no time launching a life boat and started for the *Johnson.* They had first hoped to help the crew cast off the anchor line and arrange to have a tug tow the stranded vessel into the harbor. By the time they reached the ship, the life savers knew that the seas were too high to risk sending a tug. The decision was made to scuttle the schooner to save the hull from any further damage, and then rig up another breeches buoy to bring the seven crew members safely ashore. One of the local life savers, John Everleigh, stayed aboard the *Johnson* while the others put off for shore. As the flooded ship settled to the bottom, everybody scrambled into the ropes to await rescue.

On the way back to shore, the life boat capsized in the heavy surf and life saver John Goodroe was nearly drowned. Goodroe first got entangled in the heaving line. He was gasping for air by the time he worked himself free and came back to the surface. Next Goodroe lost his grip on the overturned boat and was carried by a wave against the rocks and posts, where he was pinned, too weak to help himself. Two city police officers, identified as Patrolman Charles Miller and a Sergeant Johnson, pulled him to safety.

While the drama was going on at the pier, the other life savers were working their way into the harbor, where they fought their way through the storm and then scaled the breakwater. There, with their clothes still soaked from their spill, the men brought a cannon and the breeches buoy out on the pier with the help of a nearby farm horse. A reporter for the *Cleveland Herald* wrote: "the mortar was placed in position and the ball to which the line was attached was aimed so skillfully that Everleigh, who was up in the rigging, caught it with his foot, and this with the wind howling by in a perfect gale. It doubtless seemed a very long time to the men in the rigging, drenched with the spray, till the line on which the basket was to run was rigged up. At any rate, it did to the reporter who cooled his heels on the pier. The first one who came over was the stewardess, Mrs. Lizzie Reed, whose clothing was saturated with the spray, and who was so benumbed with cold that for a quarter of an hour she was unable to move her hands. As soon as she came ashore she was taken to the office of the night watchman of the Lake Shore pier freight house. Mr. E. E. Beir, the night watchman, prepared some hot coffee and freely gave up his own lunch to the sailors. The sailors before the mast came over first, the mate and the captain last, and finally Everleigh." The other sailors removed successfully from the *Johnson* were first mate James Olsen and sailors Charles Nielson, William Carpenter, John Garner and Herman Thiele.

That evening the town opened up to the survivors. Captain Peterson, Mrs. Reed and John Garner spent the night at the life saving station, where they were warmed with hot coffee, red liquor and warm food. The others were brought to the Vanker Hotel, where owner J. G. Drechsler treated them to food and lodging at his own expense. As the food and drink revived them, the men laughed about Mate Olsen's concern for a trunk filled with tools, clothing and personal items, for which Olsen risked his life as the ship was scuttled. They said that as the vessel was settling, he braved the heavy seas, found the trunk floating in the cabin, and threw it overboard, hoping that it would wash ashore. Later, after he was rescued, Olsen could not find the trunk. "What would a might mean feller be that a shipwrecked sailor's trunk would take?" he asked in his broken Swedish dialect.

All three ships were later raised and repaired. Their cargos of tons of iron ore, all brought to Cleveland from Escanaba, Michigan, were also salvaged.

Sources:
    Cleveland Herald, "The *Merrill* and *Minch* Beached off the East Pier," Nov. 2, "The *Sophia Minch* Released," Nov. 7, "Cast Up By the Sea," Nov. 12, 1883, news clippings, Institute for Great Lakes Research, Perrysburg, O.
    Detroit Post & Tribune, "The Schooner *Merrill* and *Sophia Minch* Ashore at Cleveland," Nov. 2, 1883, "Work on the Wrecks," Nov. 7, 1883, microfilm rolls, State Library of Michigan, Lansing, Mich.
    Greenwood, John O., "Schooner-Barge *John T. Johnson,*" Namesakes 1900-1909, Freshwater Press, Cleveland, 1987, p. 319

Aboard the *Charles N. Ryan*

The date was November 11, 1883 and a brutal winter storm was sweeping Lake Erie. The steam barge *Ohio* with the ore laden schooner *Charles N. Ryan* in tow, was caught in the midst of it. Their destination, Fairport, Ohio, was almost within sight, only fifteen miles off the starboard bow, when the gale stopped them cold. Capt. B. P. Estis, master of the *Ohio,* said the storm roaring out of the northwest hammered at the boats from the stern and created so much havoc that he was forced to turn his bow into the wind, drop the *Ryan's* tow line, and run for shelter in Pigeon Bay. Four days later, when the storm was over and the *Ohio* finally steamed into Fairport harbor, Captain Estis was sad to learn that the *Ryan* was missing. He expressed fear that the schooner was lost. Estis explained why he dropped the tow line to the schooner. "We had on sixty pounds of steam and her valves wide open, and the hawser, a heavy one and new, flattened out until it was expected to part. He said the *Ohio* "was almost slued around into the trough of the sea. The *Ryan* was doing poorly, and finally the line was cast off and she let down her anchors." Estis said that when he last saw its lights the *Ryan* "was laboring heavily."

Imagine Estis' surprise two days later when a sail was sighted off Fairport and the ship turned out to be the lost *Ryan,* finally making port. As a harbor tug brought the vessel in, it was obvious that the schooner had been in a fight. Sails hung like tattered rags. The ship was heavily coated with ice. The hull rode low in the water; evidence of flooding. Sailors were busy working the bilge pumps. They said there were three feet of water in the hold. Workers were hired to chip away the ice and unload the *Ryan's* cargo before the battered vessel was put in dry dock for repair. Even as the dock workers hustled to unload, other men were employed to keep the pumps working as the schooner was in constant danger of sinking at its moorings.

Capt. M. E. Walker, master of the *Ryan,* said the schooner first dropped its large anchor, swung its bow around into the storm, and rode the seas like a duck after the *Ohio* left him. It was later, when the wind shifted to the southwest, but the seas continued rolling from the northwest, that the trouble started. "She was worked around by the wind until she was in the trough of the northwest sea," Walker said. "Every wave went over her and flooded her decks. The main deck hatches were battered down to prevent the water getting into her hold. One of the hatches on her upper deck was washed off and the water flooded her main deck. It became necessary to bail her and keep the pumps working to save her from foundering. The pumps were manned for four days and five nights until the crew were completely exhausted."

All this time, the *Ryan* remained anchored within fifteen miles of the safety of Fairport harbor. On the sixth day, with the storm still raging, Captain Walker decided to take a chance and run for Fairport. "The crew were overworked and the constant wearing of the ship had opened her seams. She was fast making water and the mizzen sail, which had been up to steady her, had been blown to pieces." On Friday morning Walker gave the order to ship the anchor, raise sail and steer for Fairport.

The task of getting under way again was not easy. The large anchor was so embedded on the bottom of the lake that it could not be raised. Walker ordered the chain slipped away just to free the boat. As soon as that was done, the *Ryan* began drifting at the mercy of the seas and a second, smaller anchor was dropped to turn the ship back into the wind while the crew worked at getting the sails hoisted. Raising the sails was a problem because the furled canvas was covered with a thick coating of ice that had to be chipped away. As the sailors worked at chipping the ice, the schooner's small anchor dragged, causing the vessel to drift once more before the wind. "The anchor was then hove up and the *Ryan* made for the harbor under her foresail. She was close into the piers before a tug came out to her. I thought we would have to sail in," Walker said.

Sources:
    Cleveland Herald, "The *Ohio* and the Missing *Ryan,*" and "Experience of Captain Walker," Nov. 16 and Nov. 18, 1883, news clippings, Institute for Great Lakes Research, Perrysburg, O.

Oil Over Troubled Water

There is an old story that oil will calm troubled water. Capt. William H. Jones and the crew of the bark *George Sherman* found out that the remedy really works. They tried it when their ship was left floating without a rudder amidst a storm on Lake Huron on May 15, 1884.

The *Sherman* was the last ship on a tow line behind the steamer *Raleigh* and the schooner *Lucerne*. The three vessels were on their way down the lakes from Escanaba with cargoes of iron ore, when the storm struck. When off Thunder Bay the line parted and the *Sherman* was left on its own. The crew hoisted sail and continued on toward Port Huron. The rudder failed off Saginaw Bay and the ship broached. Jones tried to bring it around with the help of sail, but the storm was sweeping the lake with such power the wind blew away the jibs and square sail. Stripped of its head gear, the *Sherman* was, in a sense, a derelict being pushed by wind and sea toward certain destruction at Point aux Barques. The seas were constantly washing the decks, and the bark was taking on water. Jones wondered if it would sink before striking shore. The crew was helpless do anything to save themselves other than climb into the rigging and hang on for the ride.

The sailors remained there for hours. Night fell and with the darkness came thoughts of total helplessness and despair. No one was sure they would last until the next morning. Hours of agony, hanging in the ropes with hands numbed and muscles aching from the extreme cold, passed. Jones said he thought it was about one o'clock in the morning when one of the sailors thought of the old adage about oil calming troubled water. The man asked the captain if there was any truth to the story. Jones said he remembered hearing the same story but had never tried it. He said he was willing to try anything at this point. The sailors wiggled cautiously down from their perch, stumbled across the pitching deck, and after rummaging around in the locker, came up with a can of kerosene, used in the ship's lamps. It was poured in the water but nothing happened. Somebody grumbled that it was all an old wives tale anyway. By now their clothes were thoroughly drenched and they were shivering from the cold. Some of the crew members were ready to give up and climb back up in the rigging when someone found a barrel of linseed oil. Jones said he used a handful of oakum, which he dipped in the oil and then slowly squeezed it out over the side of the schooner. He carefully spread the oil the entire length of the ship. Like magic the oil spread out over the lake and the water grew calm. The ship stopped rolling.

Jones said he was surprised not only that the oil worked, but that it only took a small amount to do the trick. He said in all, he poured no more than twelve gallons in the water. The oil spread out for about a half mile from the *Sherman* in all directions. The bark was still riding in its own self-made sea of tranquillity at dawn, when people on shore spotted its distress flags. By then the *Sherman* had drifted farther south and was getting close to the coast near Sand Beach. The local life savers and a harbor tug were dispatched. By then the crew had most of the water in the hold pumped out and some order established on the ship.

Sources:
    Cleveland Herald, "The *George Sherman's* Experience," May 22, 1884, news clips, Institute for Great Lakes Research, Perrysburg, O.
    Master information data sheet, Institute for Great Lakes Research, Perrysburg, O.

Near Wrecking of the *Charles H. Burton*

An autumn storm was whipping Lake Erie the night of Tuesday, October 20, 1885, and the schooner *Charles A. Burton* was taking a beating. Strapped to a tow line behind the barge *L. W. Drake* and the steamer *Oregon,* the coal laden *Burton* was riding low in the water and consequently taking the gray seas over its decks. The three ships were hugging the Canadian coast as they worked their way westward toward the safety of the Detroit River. The winds tore at the ship, first from the southeast and later from the south as the night progressed. Nevertheless, Captain Kelly had the sails partly raised to take advantage of the wind at his stern and to help the steamer get its two consorts into the river and out of harms way as quickly as possible.

Disaster struck when a strong gust of wind put too much pressure on the mizzen sail and snapped the mast at the crosstrees, sending the mast, sail and rigging crashing to the deck. The falling mast took with it the foreboom, mizzenboom and gaff, and smashed a large hole in one of the ship's wooden hatch covers amidships. Other hatch covers were damaged, with some of the bars and canvass covers ripped away. Kelly was on the deck and a piece of the falling wreckage whacked him on the head and right arm. He was temporarily stunned, but not seriously injured, and was able to maintain command of his ship. That the skipper was still in command was a good thing, because the *Burton* was now in serious trouble. With holes in the hatches, the ship was taking water and in danger of sinking. With the holds filled with coal, the vessel offered little freeboard. Gallons of Lake Erie poured through the open wounds with every wave that swept the ship. The crew began working the ship's after pump, but something went wrong and the pump failed. In the meantime, there was great confusion when the wind whipped the collapsed sail around on the deck, damaging the ship's bulwarks and stanchions.

By the time Kelly was coming to his senses and assessing the damage, his mate reported three feet of water in the hold and rising. Kelly ordered the tow line cut, then turned the ship north to run before the wind to the Canadian coast. By now the wind had turned and was blowing directly from the southward. The *Burton* made it to Glasgow where it found shelter and dropped anchor. When the storm was over, the tug *A. P. Dorr* took the schooner in tow to Buffalo for repair.

Source:
    Cleveland Leader, "The *C. F. Burton* Arrives at Buffalo with Broken Masts and Torn Sails," Oct. 26, 1885, news clippings, Institute for Great Lakes Research, Perrysburg, O.

Four Days and Nights on a Wreck

The frostbitten crew stumbled from the frozen deck of the grounded schooner *A. C. Maxwell* near Goderich, Ontario, on December 9, 1885, with an incredible story of hardship and terror on Lake Huron. The men survived four days and nights adrift, enduring blizzards and temperatures that fell to near zero degrees before their ore laden ship grounded to a stop on the Canadian shore. After their rescue they told of having to constantly chip ice from the deck and work the hand-operated bilge pump without stopping to keep the ship afloat. Stripped of both sails and rudder, the *Maxwell* was a derelict, drifting about the lake at the whim of wind and wave. Captain W. Parker said the ship's fires were out, the food was gone, and he had given up all hope by the time the northwest gale developed that drove the wreck to Canada.

The *Maxwell's* troubles started early in the morning of December 5 when it got separated from the towing steam barge *V. Swain* in the midst of a winter gale somewhere off Pointe aux Barques. The two ships were making a daring final trip of the season, from Marquette to Cleveland with iron ore. Parker took a time-honored course of action. He dropped anchor and tried to ride out the storm on the open lake. The anchor caused the ship to turn its bow into the teeth of the gale and thus offer the least amount of resistance to both wind and sea. This was no ordinary storm, however. It grew in strength and after a time, the wind shifted while the seas continued to roll from the original direction. Mountainous seas hammered the ship from an angle that strained the vessel. The storm carried away the rudder and lifeboat. As the temperatures dropped, the spray coated the deck with a heavy layer of deadly ice. The wind later shifted to the northwest and the anchor dragged. Before the crew could get the ship under control the *Maxwell* broached. After this the vessel was constantly battered by seas which took a broadside shot at the wooden hull. For hours, then days the *Maxwell* drifted out of control. The seas rolled over the decks, creating more and more ice. The ship rolled so violently that no man could rest or even stand upright without being knocked down again. The hull began taking on water, mostly from the ship's scuppers, so the crew was forced to constantly man the bilge pump. The men lived in this state of horror, unable to sleep or eat, from Friday night, then all day Saturday and again on Sunday and Monday.

Parker one time ordered sails hoisted. He reasoned that his only chance of saving the ship was to use the sails to guide the vessel without the help of a rudder. He knew it was an almost hopeless thing to try, but Parker was a fighter. To do less was to give up and let the storm take him, his crew and his ship. It was a terrible task because the ice coated the decks, the sails and the ropes. The sailors spent agonizing hours chipping the ice, then using frost-stiffened hands to try to hoist the stiff canvass. It was all for naught. The gale tore the sails to shreds.

J. H. Stewart, a writer for the Sault Ste. Marie *Evening News,* recalled the event in a story he wrote in December, 1935. He said the *Maxwell* became a "helpless derelict. At first she drifted close to the American shore but a change of wind took her out again into the middle of the lake where for days she drifted back and forth until it seemed she was going to rival the 'Flying Dutchman' that sailed the south Atlantic for so many years without getting anywhere. The temperature stayed near the zero mark continually. The crew began to fear that the vessel would sink (or possibly capsize) from the great load of ice that was accumulating. At every lull the crew would sally forth with bars and axes and clear the deck and rail of tons of ice. In this way they managed to keep her

*The schooner **A. C. Maxwell** drifted for four horrible days during a December gale on Lake Huron in 1885. The crew survived great hardship. Courtesy Institute for Great Lakes Research.*

afloat for almost a week. But with their fires out, their provisions gone and with death staring them in the face from hunger and exposure they grounded one night in a northwester on the Canadian side of the lake," Stewart wrote.

The *Maxwell* came to rest on a reef near Goderich at about 4:00 AM Tuesday, December 9. The men began ringing the ship's bell. It was the only means of signaling that was available to them in the dark. The sailors were so exhausted they didn't want to wait until dawn to be rescued. Someone heard the bell and the newly established Goderich life-saving team was summoned out in the storm. That crew, led by Captain William Babb, braved high seas filled with chunks of floating ice and slush to get everybody safely ashore before daylight. The United States government, represented by Captain J. G. Kiah, superintendent of the Tenth U.S. Life Saving District, later presented the Goderich life savers with medals for their good work. The *Maxwell* was salvaged the next spring. The schooner remained on the lakes until a freak accident in 1908. The vessel was rammed by the steamer *R. W. England* while docked at Sault Ste. Marie. The collision split the *Maxwell* in two, sheering off twenty feet of its bow

Sources:

      Detroit Free Press, "Adrift Five Days," Dec. 10, 1885, microfilm rolls, State Library of Michigan, Lansing, Mich.

      Detroit Free Press, "Schooner *Maxwell* Sunk, Nov. 6, 1908, news clippings, Institute for Great Lakes Research, Perrysburg, O.

      Cleveland Leader "*Maxwell* Aground Four Miles Below Goderich-All Hands Save Ashore," and "The *Maxwell* and Crew," Dec. 10 and 11, 1885, news clippings, Institute for Great Lakes Research, Perrysburg, O.

      Master Sheet, "*Maxwell, A. C.*, Institute for Great Lakes Research, Perrysburg, O.

      Sault Ste. Marie Evening News, "Ghost Ship of Lake Huron Which Sailed 50 Years Ago Recalled by Navigation Close," Dec. 13, 1935, news clippings, Institute for Great Lakes Research, Perrysburg, O.

Becalmed and Sinking

If it wasn't for the fact that it was a valuable ore laden ship in extreme danger of being lost, the situation could almost have been laughable. The schooner *A. Boody* of Detroit was lying becalmed and sinking in northern Lake Michigan, within sight of Great Beaver Island. A sounding revealed that the water below was about one hundred and twenty feet, which meant that if the *Boody* sank there, it probably could not be raised again. Shallow water was nearby. The exhausted crew was taking turns at the pump, doing everything possible to keep the ship afloat until the wind returned.

The *Boody* was sailing from Escanaba, Michigan, to Cleveland on August 12, 1886, when the wind died. Living on a becalmed sailing ship requires patience. There is nothing the crew can do except wait for the wind to return. In the *Boody's* case, someone noticed about 4:00 AM that the ship had sprung a leak. Investigation revealed four feet of water in the hold. The pump only seemed to keep the flooding in check. No matter how hard they pumped, the sailors couldn't get the ship dry again. In fact, the water gained. The only hope was wind so the *Boody* could make a dash to Beaver Island. No wind came.

The men pumped from the time the leak was discovered until four o'clock the following afternoon and they were worn out. The day was hot and steamy. Callused hands were blistered and sore. Muscles ached. They worked in shifts. Each man fell to the deck in a semi-stupor as he was relieved at his post. At that hour the captain decided to give up and abandon ship. His men were too tired to go on. He ordered the yawl boat lowered from the davits, and told the men to put their clothes and other personal things in the boat. Then, just as they were about to cast off, someone spotted smoke from an approaching tugboat. Encouraged by a chance of still saving the *Boody*, the crew members returned to their jobs at the pump. They worked until the tug *Martin Swain* pulled alongside. New workers took over the pumping chore while the tired sailors fell away exhausted. By now the schooner was nearly sunk to the decks. It was so low in the water everybody thought it would sink. The *Swain* connected a hawser and in about an hour had the *Boody* pulled into shallow water near the island. There it grounded on a sandy bottom.

*The **A. Boody** narrowly escaped sinking on Lake Michigan. Institute for Great Lakes Research Photo*

The *Swain* sailed off to Mackinac Island, where it picked up a steam pump, then returned and put it to work on the schooner's deck. By the next day the ship was pumped out and under tow, bound for Cleveland. The steam pump kept the *Boody* afloat for the remainder of the trip. At Cleveland the cargo was removed and the vessel went into dry dock for repair.

The *Boody* measured one hundred thirty-seven feet. It was built at Toledo in 1863 and remained on the lakes under the names *Boody* and later *E. A. Fulton,* the latter under Canadian registry, until about 1907.

Sources:

 Detroit Free Press, "The Schooner *Boody* Sunk at the Beavers,",", Aug. 14, 1886, microfilm rolls, State Library of Michigan, Lansing, Mich.

 Detroit Free Press, "The Schooner *Boody's* Narrow Escape From Sinking in Lake Michigan—A Hard-Worked Crew," Aug. 17, 1886, news clipping, Institute for Great Lakes Research, Perrysburg, O.

 Master data file, Institute for Great Lakes Research, Perrysburg, O.

Hopelessly Adrift in a Gale

When the revenue cutter *Commodore Perry* steamed into Buffalo harbor on October 17, 1886, it had a bedraggled appearing schooner, the *Red White & Blue,* in tow. People gathered along the waterfront to witness the schooner and hear the story of what happened to its crew during a gale that raged across Lake Erie four days earlier. The ship's canvas hung in shreds. Windows were smashed. Things on the deck were either missing or in disarray. The schooner moved against its tow line in odd, twisting motions, giving testimony to a missing rudder. The ship also listed from water and a shifted cargo of coal in its holds.

The master of the *Red White & Blue,* a man identified only as Captain Shaw, told about the ordeal on October 14 that almost sank his ship. He praised his crew for not giving up in their battle to keep the vessel afloat. The sailors all knew that if the schooner sank, they could not live. The *Red White & Blue* and schooner *Newsboy* left Buffalo together on

*The **Red White & Blue** is displayed as a barkentine in this artist's concept. The ship was rigged as a schooner when it was almost lost in a Lake Erie blow in 1886. Courtesy Institute for Great Lakes Research.*

October 13; both ships under tow behind the tug *Crusader*. The storm struck them in mid-lake the next day. Captain Shaw said the wind blew from the south so the *Crusader* moved close to the Ohio coast to keep in the lee of the land. Even there the gale put a strain on the three ships. When off Conneaut, Ohio, the tow line to the *Newsboy* separated. The schooner's crew raised sail and turned back for Buffalo. Soon after that, the tug released its line to the *Red White & Blue* and also turned back for the safety of Buffalo's harbor.

Shaw was a bold master who had confidence in himself and his ship. Instead of following the others, he ordered his crew to set sail and ride the southerly wind eastward toward the Detroit River. Things went well until 4:00 PM when the gale shifted to the west. After that, Shaw saw that it was futile to try to beat against the wind and sea. He turned northeast toward the safety of Long Point. The schooner took a terrible beating as the storm grew in its fury. "About nine o'clock, when the gale was at its height, a great sea struck the vessel's stern, tore off the steering gear box and unshipped the wheel. She was jumping furiously and with great difficulty an iron tiller was attached to the rudder post," Shaw said. "The tiller soon gave way and the ship was completely at the mercy of the wind and sea." The schooner broached into the trough of the seas, then began a violent rolling motion. To make matters worse, a hole in the hull where the rudder had been attached was leaking. The crew had to man the bilge pumps constantly to keep ahead of the water. As they worked, each man was in danger of being swept overboard by the seas that washed across the deck. To protect themselves the sailors tied themselves to the ship.

"A great sea swept over the starboard rail and into the foresail, carrying the canvas away as if it were gauze. The main and mizzen sails were also torn into shreds, as well as two jibs and a stay sail. Seas washed six or eight feet over the vessel's side and carried away some of the bulwarks. Booms, canvas and portable things were tumbled about the deck." a story in the *Detroit Free Press* said. As they struggled to keep their ship afloat, Shaw said he and some of the other sailors were sometimes knocked to the deck by the violent seas. Sometimes the only thing that saved them from being washed overboard was their lifelines. They were left bruised and sore from the constant battering.

"For eight hours, through the dead of night, the ship drifted in that awful storm, not knowing when they might be dashed to pieces or engulfed," the story said. At 2:00 AM Shaw ordered the anchors dropped, hoping that the schooner was drifted into shallow enough water for the hooks to grasp bottom. Alas, the anchor chains were too short. The *Red White & Blue* drifted another three hours. It was at about 5:00 AM that the anchors found solid rock off Dunkirk, New York. At last, the schooner was turned around with its bow pointed into the teeth of the storm.

A check in the hold found two and one-half feet of water. The sailors continued to take turns working the pump while Shaw raised distress signals. When dawn came, he saw that the vessel was anchored about four miles off shore. At about the same time, people of Dunkirk said they saw the schooner anchored off shore. Apparently nobody put a glass on the ship and saw the distress flags flying off the mast. That was unfortunate, because if they had, a tug might have been dispatched to bring the leaking vessel to safety much sooner. As it was, another twenty-four hours passed before the steamer *Arizona* came on the wreck and took it in tow to Erie, Pennsylvania. By then, the crew was totally exhausted. From there, the *Perry* brought the vessel back to Buffalo.

Source:
      Detroit Free Press, "Rough Experience of the Schooner *Red White and Blue* in Thursday's Big Blow," Oct. 16, 1886, microfilm file, State Library of Michigan, Lansing, Mich.
      Detroit Post and Tribune, "Frightful Experience of the *Red White and Blue* Thursday Night," Oct. 18, 1886, microfilm file, State Library of Michigan, Lansing, Mich.

The Line of Life

The situation appeared hopeless for the eight sailors on the schooner-barge *Polynesia.* As night fell, the barge, in tow behind the steamer *Raleigh,* was left in a wrecked and sinking condition by a wild nor'wester. Nobody on the *Raleigh* believed that the barge could last until daylight.

The gale of Sunday, October 23, 1887, had pounced like a lion on the two ships as they made their way across Lake Michigan on the final leg of what had been a long haul from Buffalo to Chicago. The storm first tore the *Polynesia's* sails to shreds, then hammered at the barge from astern with such force that the coal laden vessel sprung a leak. A writer for the *Chicago Inter Ocean* said: "A furious sea was on, washing over both vessels, and the decks of the barge were soon totally submerged, the water shipped being on a level with the top of the deck bulwarks. For four hours the steamer and her disabled consort continued dragging in toward the west shore. When night fell the *Raleigh* put to, and Capt. A. H. Reed, (the *Raleigh's* master) concluded to await daylight." It turned out to be a most anxious wait for the crews of both ships. That night the storm grew stronger and the seas got higher. The *Raleigh's* mainmast head and mizzen topmast were carried away. It was discovered that the steamer also was leaking and even with steam powered pumps, the water in the hold gained. To keep the two vessels from getting blown back out into mid-lake, the steamer's engines were operating at full steam ahead, her bow turned into the teeth of the gale. Sailors on the streamer could not see the lights from the *Polynesia,* although the two-hundred-foot line leading from the *Raleigh* to the barge remained taunt, stretching out into the darkness dead astern, indicating that the barge was still there and still afloat.

On the *Polynesia,* Capt. John W. Kerr and his crew knew they were on the brink of death. All eight sailors huddled together near the life boat while the seas rolled over the partly submerged wreck, drenching them constantly. The men had not eaten for more than a day and they were weak from both hunger and the constant exposure to the elements. Kerr knew it would be suicide to launch the life boat and try to escape the sinking barge that night. He understood, as did Captain Reed in the steamer standing nearby, that their only chance was if the barge lasted until morning.

The *Inter Ocean* story explained the drama: "The *Polynesia* lay in the trough of the sea with her cabin roof flush with the water. Forward the seas were washing over her, and her head was kept above water only by the tow line, which was subjected to so great a strain that it was momentarily threatened to part under the pressure. Captain Kerr and his crew were kept aft on the deck. No one, exhausted as all hands were, thought of sleep. They all knew that there was but a towline between themselves and eternity. The vessel's yawl was swung off on her stern davits ready to be launched should the hull settle aft."

As the night progressed, conditions continued to deteriorate on the *Raleigh* as well. "With four feet of water in her hold, the steam barge could not last much longer. Her engineer had reported at short intervals throughout the night that he could not hold her engines together unless she was freed of the line," the *Inter Ocean* story said. As conditions got worse, Reed's worried crew pleaded with him to cut the tow line to the barge so they could save themselves. Some of the sailors may have thought that Reed, then only twenty-five years of age, was too young and inexperienced to be the pilot of a steamer. Reed stood firm. "I thought it was murder in the first degree to let go," he later explained. Then, at around 6:00 AM, the long awaited daybreak arrived. "When the eastern horizon revealed the dawn of day the scene was a wild one," the news story said. "About the vessel's sides, as far as the eye could sea, the sea was foam-lashed. The vessel was lying head to the land on her beam ends, and could be seen sinking inch-by-inch. It was ten minutes past six o'clock when Captain Kerr and the crew of the *Polynesia* got into the yawl boat. The *Raleigh's* commander was aft on the taffrail and saw them safe in the little boat. The latter pulled astern of the *Polynesia* about forty yards and none too soon. She settled down stern first and the captain of the *Raleigh* called for an ax. At one blow the hawser was severed. The *Polynesia,* freed, settled down aft. As the next sea struck her she rose above the turbulent waters forward, and sank out of sight, the waters closing over her with a loud noise."

Taken safely aboard the *Raleigh* that morning were Captain Kerr, mate Jesse Joseph, and sailors William Goff, Fred Hancock, Charles Smythe, Charles Merke, Richard Gibson and Henry McCriskin. Needless to say, Captain Reed was highly praised for his actions. The *Polynesia,* built at Bay City only two years earlier, measured two hundred four feet in length. It was carrying nearly two thousand tons of coal when it sank about twenty miles east of Sheboygan, Wisconsin.

Source:
       Beers, J. H. & Co., Chicago, History of the Great Lakes Illustrated, Vol. I , biography of Capt. A. H. Reed, p 56, and Vol. II, report of the loss of the *Polynesia,* p 750, published 1899.
       Chicago Inter Ocean, "Foundering of the *Polynesia,*" Oct. 26, 1887, news clippings, Institute for Great Lakes Research, Perrysburg, O.

The Surfman's Tale

It was October 1, 1888, and a northwest gale had been building all day. One-by-one a fleet of ships dropped anchor behind the newly constructed mile-wide breakwater at Sand Beach, Michigan, to escape the fury looming on Lake Huron. Charles Ferris was one of the young surfmen stationed at the government life saving station there. Years later, in a letter to Charles Quay, a prominent Forester, Michigan businessman, Ferris told about standing the afternoon watch and seeing the steam barge *Lowell* beat its way toward him from the south. The ship was laboring hard against the gale but making almost no headway because it had six coal laden barges in tow. "She was being badly punished by the seas and appeared to be in trouble. As I watched I could see the barges being cut adrift, one-by-one."

Captain George W. Plough, the man in charge at the station, said the *Lowell* made it through the harbor gap, but it left the six barges, identified as the *Lily May, St. Clair, Oliver Cromwell, William Young, Seagull* and *Magnet*, anchored at the mercy of the storm. The steamer's engine didn't have the power to pull its charges against the elements to safety. The *Lowell's* skipper asked a harbor tug to try to bring the drifting barges in, but the tugboat captain refused to leave the safety of the harbor. Plough took the life savers out in a late afternoon check of the condition of the stranded vessels. "The *St. Clair* was loaded with coal and we knew her to be unseaworthy. We wanted her captain (C. H. Jones of Bay City) to abandon her, but he would not do so. We stayed with him for about an hour. It was raining and cold and we became chilled. We again called to the captain and asked him to leave the vessel but he refused to do so. Both anchors were holding and Captain Jones was disposed to stay with the vessel," wrote Ferris. "He said all he had was tied up in her and he would stick with her till the last. After we saw that it was impossible to get the captain or any of his crew to go ashore, Captain Plough asked for the girl (the *St. Clair's* cook, Julia Greawreath of Sebewaing, Michigan) but for some reason she wouldn't come with us. We then informed Captain Jones that if he needed us to burn a torch as a signal. . . After a long and back-breaking pull into the teeth of the gale we finally made it through the gap, drenched and nearly exhausted. So we went to our station and now it was blowing a living gale, and increasing by the minute.

"It was my watch down at the end of the pier. In going to my station I had to watch and run between the madly rushing seas which were sweeping over the breakwater. I had not been at my post very long when I saw a torch on the *St. Clair*. I worked myself back to the station and reported to Captain Plough," Ferris said. By now, the surfmen were extremely tired, and the prospect of taking the surf boat back out in that storm was troublesome. The surfmen knew they were really going to be putting their lives on the line this time. Ferris said some of the men gave their money and personal things to Captain Plough's wife before they left. They had thoughts of not coming back alive. Surfboats in 1888 were wide, relatively stable craft, measuring about thirty feet in length. They were open boats, without engines, although they were usually equipped with a mast and sail. The main source of power was by oar. Each boat was manned by nine surfmen, eight of them there to row and one man to work the tiller. It took much courage to take such a craft out into a storm like the one sweeping Lake Huron that night.

"We manned the lifeboat in the worst storm any of us had ever seen. As we pulled across the harbor the sky was pitch black and the wind was whistling through the rigging of the boats lying in shelter. After passing through the gap we hit the storm in all its fury. The seas were coming from all directions and it was a difficult task to keep the life boat headed in the right direction. We finally came up to the *St. Clair* and endeavored to pull under her stern in order to remove the crew to the lifeboat. We had to get close enough to take them off one-by-one and still keep far enough off so our boat wouldn't be stove in by the larger boat. One minute we would be riding high above her and the next she would rise on a huge wave and be high above us. Several times we narrowly missed disaster when her stern came down, just missing us it seemed by inches. The girl jumped first and then the men one at a time, with Captain Jones being the last to come aboard.

"We left the harbor at seven o'clock and it was 11:00 PM when we were ready to pull away from the *St. Clair*. The seas were now so high and the wind so strong that it was impossible for us to pull back to the harbor. There was only one thing to do. That was to run with the storm and let the seas and the wind carry us south toward the shelter of the St. Clair River. That would mean a run of sixty miles but there was no other way. And perhaps by morning the gale would lessen. As we squared away and headed down the lake our job was to keep the lifeboat on a true course, running with the seas. To allow her to get crosswise into the seas would allow her to broach and throw us all into the water. Our rudder was soon struck by a huge sea and carried away. Captain Plough shouted orders to the crew that we would have to steer the boat by port and starboard oarsmen. . . we shipped many (large waves) and our boat filled with water five or six times, but she was a self-bailer and emptied herself each time. She behaved very well while running with the seas.

"One big sea caught us and put out our light so Captain Plough couldn't see the compass. He called for matches and just one man had a few dry ones. After some trouble we got the lantern lighted and got back on course. To get off course was to court disaster. To get too far off to port would invite broaching and to get too far off to starboard could bring us too close to the rocky shore where anything could happen. The wind kept blowing with unabated fury and it seemed like all the demons of hell had been let loose. All of us were drenched many times as the seas and spray continued to sweep over the boat. We were all near exhaustion and suffering with the cold. It seemed like the night would never end. Keeping the light going so the captain could read the compass also became quite a chore. Two or three of the men were given a chance to hold the lantern, but in turn they gave it up as their hands got so cold and numb they could no longer hold it. Then the girl took it and didn't give it up until daylight. All through the night she kept the lantern safe and sheltered the light from the wind and the seas. Never once did she complain of the cold.

"Captain Plough directed us to keep looking for a light, either from a boat or from shore. But we didn't see one from the time we left the *St. Clair* until just about daylight. Then at about 7:00 AM the captain sighted the Port Sanilac light. He wanted to get the crew ashore as soon as possible as he feared they would perish from the cold, so he decided to attempt a landing. It had now been eight hours since we left the *St. Clair* and we had made thirty miles, just half the distance to the shelter of the river. To continue on with an exhausted crew was impossible. There is a limit to human endurance and we had reached that point. After twelve hours of continually fighting the storm, we had reached the end.

"At Port Sanilac there was very little shelter. Just a dock about five hundred feet long where the steamers landed, built partly of log cribs and partly of piling. The captain decided to round the dock and attempt a landing on the south or leeward side and take advantage of what little shelter there was. The residents of Port Sanilac had been informed during the night and knew the lifeboat was headed down the lake. Scores of people were on the dock to witness what happened and many were prepared to be of assistance. It was lucky for me that they were or I would not be here to tell this tale. We headed for the light. The dock and all the people came plainly into view. As we neared shore we were pushed forward by the madly rushing breakers which kept getting more wicked. Captain Plough ordered the oil tank opened and if it helped I cannot say. Our lifeboat was about thirty feet long and time after time those breakers would start astern and coil clear over the boat and would never wet the crew. I looked up and it was just like a falls. I expected to see the lifeboat go end over end a number of times, but we came through all this. However, just as we were rounding the dock the boat was struck by a tremendous breaker and she rolled down on her beam ends. I did not realize it until I was under the boat. I put my hands up against something and pushed myself down. I bobbed up quickly and found myself some distance from the boat. I could see she was on her side and some men were clinging to her but I had to go where the breakers and the back wash and the undertow were taking me. I was completely exhausted and it seemed at times that the breakers would smother me. I got in closer to shore and I thought I might touch bottom with my foot just for a rest, but when I tried it, a breaker went clear over me. I was now becoming very weak. I saw a man coming toward me from shore with a rope tied around his waist and the other end was held by people on shore. He shouted to me and said there was a channel between us and he couldn't get out any farther but I thought that he could get me after another breaker sent me in. Another breaker came roaring in and that is the last thing that I remember. When I was revived I was at the lighthouse. Afterward they told me they worked on me for four hours. Then they told me the name of the man who had pulled me from the water. He was Coly (Colin C.) McGregor and he was the dock agent." Ferris was one of the lucky ones. Captain Jones and four crew members from the *St. Clair* were drowned. The others were Miss Greawreath, Henry Anderson of Australia, Louis Furtaw of Bay City, Michigan, and George McFarlane of Cleveland, Ohio. Their bodies washed ashore later in the day about two miles south of the pier. They were laid out in the township hall at Port Sanilac. The next day the remains of Captain Jones and Furtaw were sent to Bay City for burial. The others were buried in the Port Sanilac cemetery. The late Oliver Raymond, the town historian, said he had a theory that the reason the surfmen all survived the accident was because they were wearing life jackets. It also may have been that the surfers were all trained for this kind of emergency. Except for Ferris, the others were all hanging onto the side of the overturned boat when they washed ashore. They just rode it through the surf to safety. In addition to Plough, the rest of the life saving crew were J. E. Tucker, Eugene Brown, Charles Lebow, William Small, Edward Prescott, Frank Ocha and William Smith.

The *St. Clair* went on the rocks south of Sand Beach near Rock Falls and broke up. About fifty tons of coal were later recovered. The *Cromwell* also dragged its anchor and the captain ran it aground. The crew escaped in the ship's yawl and the vessel was later stripped and left as a total wreck.

Sources:
  Chicago Inter Ocean, "Wrecked by the Winds," Oct. 3, 1888, news clippings, Institute for Great Lakes Research, Perrysburg, O.
  Detroit Free Press, "The Life Boat Upset," Oct. 3, 1888, news clippings, Institute for Great Lakes Research, Perrysburg, O.
  Ferris, Charles, "The Wreck of the Barge *St. Clair,* a personal account written to the late Charles Quay of Forester, Mich., July 1, 1947.
  Harbor Beach Times, Oct. 2, 1888, from bound newspapers in city clerk's office, Harbor Beach, Mich.

The *Lathrop* Saga

When it was over, Capt. James Glenn, master of the scow *Lathrop,* grinned and said he was never frightened. "We had a hard time of it, but I just kept my head and let her go with the wind," he explained. The owners said they never expected to see the crew of the old wooden hulled vessel alive after a winter gale toppled the *Lathrop's* masts and cast the vessel helplessly adrift on the seething waters of Saginaw Bay.

It happened on November 19, 1891, when the *Lathrop,* loaded with one hundred tons of coal, and two other barges, the *Russian* and *Light Guard,* were being towed across Lake Huron to Alpena behind the steamer *Garden City.* The storm caught them in the widest and most dangerous part of the lake. The *Lathrop's* troubles dropped on the crew without warning. As the wind howled overhead, the shrouds of the foremast snapped from the strain and the sail, ropes and tackle fell over the port rail. Once the ropes began breaking loose, it put extra tension on the main mast, and that mast broke with a loud crack and toppled over the port side, pulling the rest of the foremast with it. Glenn said the foremast was ripped up by the base, which tore up part of the deck.

Nobody was hurt. Everything happened so quickly, the sailors found themselves standing awestruck for a few moments. They were forced into action fast enough, however, after Captain Glenn assessed the damage and began snapping orders. The drag from all of the sails, masts, ropes and pulleys that had fallen in the water, but were still attached to the ship, strained and then parted the tow line to the *Garden City.* Glenn and his crew found themselves adrift in a ship without power on a violent gale-swept lake.

In retrospect, Glenn found himself boasting about the way he escaped. "It was the third time I've been demasted so I was getting used to it," he joked. He directed his men to use axes to cut the fallen spars, ropes and sails free. Next they used canvas from one of the hatch covers to make a small sail and raise it over the forecastle cabin. It wasn't much, but the little sail, carefully mounted on the bow, caught enough wind to turn the vessel around. Slowly the *Lathrop* rode before the southwest wind toward the Canadian coast. Giant seas fanned by the storm repeatedly rolled over the stern, drenching the cabins and keeping crew members wet and cold.

Glenn said it was a long and uncomfortable trip. Two days later the scow drifted to Manitoulin Island where a safe anchorage was found. By then the food was gone. The islanders, however, were quick to help. Glenn said people there brought a fine meal out to the ship on Sunday. The *Lathrop* was found a few days later by the *Frank W.*, one of two Alpena tugs hired to search for the wayward scow.

Sources:
    Alpena Argus, Nov. 25, 1891, microfilm rolls, State Library of Michigan, Lansing, Mi.
    Detroit Free Press, Nov. 24, 1891, microfilm rolls, State Library of Michigan, Lansing, Mi.

Lashed to the Mast

The gale packed sixty-mile-per-hour winds and drove other ships to destruction when it swept Lake Erie on October 14, 1893, but the schooner *Mont Blanc* and its frightened crew of eight emerged as survivors. Their story, as told by Capt. Patrick J. Cain in the *Detroit Evening News* three days later, paints a stark picture of raw terror. "When the wind began blowing forty miles an hour I thought we struck a hurricane and believed all was over with us," Cain said. "When (the wind increased) to sixty miles an hour I was in even worse shape and then believed we were going down any minute. The seas washed over the boat and drenched us to the skin."

Captain Cain, who lived in Detroit, sailed the schooner regularly between Detroit, Toledo and Buffalo, hauling mostly grain to the eastern ports. His wife, Lizzie, frequently traveled with him and was aboard the *Mont Blanc* on the day of the storm. It was unclear if she was counted as a member of the crew or traveling as a guest of the captain. The Buffalo *Sunday Morning News* said the schooner left Detroit for Buffalo on Thursday, October 12, and was somewhere off Long Point when the gale first struck late on Friday.

Cain said the rain pelted the decks like a shower of shot and the lookout could not see a hundred feet ahead. The sails were reefed and the ship was battened down for the blow, which apparently came out of the northwest. "We were away up above Long Point. It was impossible to make that harbor to get out of the fury of the storm, and I headed the boat to Buffalo. I took in as much canvas as I thought advisable and let her go." He said the rudder failed, the hull sprung a leak, and the listing ship drifted out-of-control across the lake.

When not working the pumps, the captain said the crew lashed themselves to the masts to keep from being washed overboard by the great seas which carried away anything not bolted down. Mrs. Cain also was driven to the deck after the seas flooded the cabin where she first sought shelter. When she stepped on the deck, she was caught by a wave and almost carried overboard. Cain and an unidentified sailor caught her. "I tied her to a post and then devoted myself to saving the vessel if I could. I knew if I kept the boat headed for Buffalo there would be a ghost of a chance of us being picked up by a tug in the harbor. We were almost played out when we caught sight of Buffalo. The waves were dashing over the breakwater and we were almost upon it before I realized where we were. It was raining so heavily objects could not be seen one hundred feet ahead." To keep from hitting the breakwater, Cain ordered the schooner's anchor's dropped. They held and the boat turned its bow around for the first time into the seas, giving the drenched sailors a small amount of relief. Cain knew, however, that time was running out. In spite of the crew's work at the pump, the water was gaining in the hold. The *Mont Blanc* had taken on an ominous list. Cain worried that the ship was sinking.

The schooner was noticed by the people in Buffalo and help was dispatched. Onlookers crowded the harbor front, braving the storm, to watch the drama. Two harbor tugs steamed to the stricken vessel, but then discovered that the storm had carried away the schooner's tow line. The tugs lacked hawsers of their own and could do nothing to help. Next, Capt. Patrick Lynn brought his powerful tug *Cascade* into the scene. The *Cascade* carried a big hawser, which Lynn hooked successfully to the bow of the *Mont Blanc*. The schooner was soon in the harbor and moored in the Blackwell canal. It sank fifteen minutes later. Cain was quick to praise Lynn for bringing his ship to safety as quickly as he did. "If it was not for Captain Lynn and his tug, the *Cascade,* I guess we would all be at the bottom of the lake now," he said.

Source:
   Detroit Evening News, "Lashed to the Mast," Oct. 17, 1893, microfilm file, State Library of Michigan, Lansing, Mich.

Saga At Pictured Rocks

When the schooner *Elma* broke away from the steamer *P. H. Birkhead* during a Lake Superior gale in the fall of 1895 then drifted ashore at a Michigan jagged coast known as Pictured Rocks, the crew found itself in a serious dilemma. Anyone fortunate enough to visit Pictured Rocks by boat on a calm day knows that the area is a spectacular rock formation rising several hundred feet straight up out of the water. It is a nice place for tourists to visit, but the wrong place to be stranded on a grounded, half-sunk wooden ship in the midst of a storm on Superior. The crew of the *Elma* was faced with a decision between staying on their vessel, which was getting pounded to kindling, or fleeing through a killer surf and trying to find shelter on that rocky precipice.

The *Elma* and schooners *Chester B. Jones* and *Commodore* were on a tow line behind the *Birkhead.* They were all traveling northwest after clearing the locks at Sault Ste. Marie, when the storm with winds out of the southeast caught them off Whitefish Point on Saturday, September 28. As the gale increased, the *Birkhead* turned to run for shelter on the west side of Whitefish Point. The turn put too much of a strain on the tow line and all three schooners broke away from the steamer. Both the *Jones* and *Commodore* made sail and ran off before the wind. The *Jones* survived the gale but it was nearly wrecked while anchored off Whitefish Point. The *Commodore* got safely back to Sault Ste. Marie. The *Birkhead* picked up a new tow line from the *Elma.* The *Elma's* master,

Captain Thurston, explained what happened: "After getting our line again, the *Birkhead* headed up the lake, with the hope of getting in shelter under Grand Island, but when near Pictured Rocks, the tow line again parted, and our steering gear broke. We were wholly at the mercy of the sea, which was growing every minute. The *Elma* rolled so hard in the trough of the sea that she jumped the masts out, and the rigging carried away. The schooner then waterlogged and every wave swept the deck. The crew worked hard at the pumps until the schooner struck a rock about one hundred feet from the shore at Miner's Castle. This was Sunday afternoon."

The situation looked impossible. Thurston said the wreck was pounding to pieces under the feet of the crew. Waves constantly swept the deck, threatening to carry the sailors away to certain death. The captain's wife and three-year-old son were with him on the *Elma*, which made things even more difficult. There was no place for anybody to go to get out of the water. Even the masts and rigging were gone. The normal escape would have been on the ship's yawl boat, but the giant seas slamming against the blunt rock-faced bluff only one hundred feet away spelled certain suicide. What was needed was a breeches buoy, or at least a life line strung between the shore and the wreck. There was no one on shore to offer to help string such a line, so crew member George M. Johnson of Chicago volunteered to make a run for the bluff. He took the yawl and got to the bluff, but not before the yawl was smashed to pieces in the surf. When he crawled still alive on the rocks, Johnson realized to his horror that he had lost his end of the precious rope line. Now he was stranded alone on the open rock bluff, the life boat was wrecked, and the rest of the crew was still trapped on the wreck.

Sailor Rudolph Yack of Mt. Clemens, Michigan, volunteered to swim to shore with a rope tied around his waist. He argued that he was a strong swimmer and that if he got into serious trouble, his comrades could pull him back aboard the *Elma*. Yack was killed in the attempt. The surf bashed him so hard against the rocks that his comrades thought he probably died instantly. When they tried to pull him back, they discovered that the rope had become untied. Meanwhile, conditions on the wreck were getting desperate. Thurston said the hull was taking such a pounding that he was convinced the ship would break up. Once that happened, there was little chance for anyone to escape alive. Somehow a rope line had to be gotten ashore to George Johnson. Different ideas were tried. Ropes were tied to various floating objects and allowed to drift up to the bluff, where Johnson sought to retrieve them. Finally, just before dark, Johnson succeeded in getting his hands on the elusive end of the rope. By then, however, it was too late for anything more to be tried. The sailors spent a terrifying night on the wreck wondering if they would still be alive in the morning. Thurston said: "Johnson kept hold of the line, and all night paced a narrow ledge of rock until daylight. We then escaped to the rocks by fastening one end of a line around our bodies, and being pulled up by those on the rocks. My three-year-old son, however, was kept dry by drawing the line from the rocks to the boat taut, and rigging a traveler on it. A few blankets and two loaves of bread were also brought ashore. By hard climbing and the use of the lines, we managed to climb to a partially sheltered ledge of the rocks two hundred feet above the water. There we built a fire and remained until Tuesday morning when the storm abated. We climbed down from the place of refuge and built a raft to get provisions from the wreck."

The steamer *Birkhead,* in the meantime, had been standing by near Grand Island, watching the *Elma* go to pieces in the storm. The crew of the steamer assumed that the crew of the schooner was lost. The light house keeper at Grand Island was sent over in a small boat to look for the bodies. Imagine his surprise when he found the sailors busy building a raft at the base of the cliff.

Sources:
    Chicago Inter Ocean, "Cast Upon a Ledge," Oct. 2, 1895, news clippings, Institute for Great Lakes Research, Perrysburg, O.
    Detroit Free Press, "Saved!" Oct. 2, 1895, news clippings, Institute for Great Lakes Research, Perrysburg, O.
    Duluth News Tribune, "Crew of the *Elma* Saved," Oct. 2, 1895, news clippings, Institute for Great Lakes Research, Perrysburg, O.

*The schooner **Jennie Weaver** was a lucky ship. It sailed the Great Lakes for thirty-seven years, experiencing few mishaps. Stephen Donahue collection.*

Lucky Ship *Jennie Weaver*

The schooner *Jennie Weaver* was a familiar sight to people who lived in Michigan port towns along lower Lake Huron at about the turn of the century. Measuring a modest seventy-nine feet in length, the two-master was far from imposing when it passed. Still, the *Weaver* had graceful lines and was considered by many to be the perfect model of a tall ship on the Great Lakes. Because of its size it was able to duck in and out of the entrances to small lake towns with ease. During the thirty-seven years it sailed, from the year of its launch in South Haven, Michigan in 1882, until the time it was abandoned as unfit for service at Port Huron in 1919, the *Jennie Weaver* was a most lucky ship. Its lone brush with disaster occurred during a storm on Lake Huron on September 4, 1914.

The boat was heavily laden with lumber, traveling from Alpena to Sarnia, when the gale struck and the *Weaver* sprung a leak. Trouble came as the crew was jibbing canvas abreast of the Point aux Barques light. The leak was serious because in no time the schooner filled to the decks. It didn't sink because it was filled with wood, but the crew, which included the captain's wife, spent a few wet and uncomfortable hours.

There is no place to keep dry on a waterlogged ship in a storm. The rigging leading up the masts is often where sailors go, but even there, they are constantly doused by spray from the seas pounding the deck of the ship below their feet.

Captain Fisher was a good sailor. He took advantage of the wind at his stern, and left enough sail set to push the *Weaver* along on a southerly course toward Harbor Beach, the nearest port of safety. When off Forest Bay, a small community located a few miles north of Harbor Beach, the *Weaver's* distress signals were spotted. Word was telegraphed ahead to the Harbor Beach life savers, and a boat was dispatched. Also sent was a fish tug, the *E.M.B.A.*, which took the schooner in tow. After the storm abated, the *Weaver* was towed to Sarnia by the Port Huron based tug *Sport*. There it was unloaded, and taken to dry dock for repair.

Sources:

    Detroit Free Press, "*Jennie Weaver* Mishap," Sept. 5, 1914, microfilm rolls, State Library of Michigan, Lansing, Mich.

    Harbor Beach Times, "The *Jennie Weaver*," Sept. 11, 1914, news clippings stored at city clerk's office, Harbor Beach municipal building.

Vessel Index

Nautical Terms for Tall Ships

Abaft: Toward the stern.

Abeam: On the side of the vessel amidships, or at right angles.

Aboard: Within or on board the vessel.

About: To go in an opposite tack.

Abreast: Alongside.

Adrift: Broken from moorings.

Afore: Forward.

Aft: Near the stern.

Aground: Touching on the bottom.

Aloft: Above the deck.

Amidships: The center of the vessel.

Anchor: An iron weight which holds a vessel when dropped to the bottom.

Avast: To stop.

Backstays: Rigging running from the masthead to the vessel's side, slanting a little aft or to the deck near the stern.

Ballast: Heavy material such as iron, lead or even water placed in the bottom of a ship to keep it steady.

Beams: Strong pieces of timber stretching across the vessel to support the decks.

Beam Ends: When a vessel is tipped so that its beams are included toward the vertical.

Beating: Going toward the direction of the wind by alternate tacks.

Becalm: To intercept the wind. A sailing ship standing without wind.

Before the wind: A sailing ship traveling with the wind from astern.

Below: Under the deck.

Bilge: The outer part of a ship's hull located near the keel.

By the board: When the masts of a vessel fall over the side.

Bow: The front part of a vessel.

Bow Line: A rope leading forward from the leech of a square sail used to keep the leech well out when sailing close hauled.

Bowsprint: A large, strong spar standing from the bow of a vessel.

Bring To: Stopping a sailing vessel by bringing its head into the wind.

Broach To: To slew around when running before the wind.

Broadside: The whole side of a vessel.

Bulkhead: Partition in the hold of a vessel designed to keep water from filling the hold in case of accident.

Bulwarks: Wood work around a vessel above deck.

Buntlines: Ropes used for raising sails.

Buoy: A floating, anchored device used to mark shoals and other obstructions in the water.

Butt: The end of a plank where it unites with the end of another.

Capsize: To overturn.

Capstan: A machine on the deck used for heaving heavy objects such as the anchor.

Close-Hauled: Sailing as close to the wind as possible.

Coamings: Raised work around the hatches to prevent water from going in the hold.

Compass: An instrument which shows the course of a vessel.

Cross-Trees: Metal or wood bars joined crosswise on a mast to support sails and rigging.

Davit: A device used to store and launch life boats.

Dead Lights: Cabin windows.

Deck: The planked floor of a vessel.

Derelict: A vessel adrift and forsaken on the high seas.

Even Keel: When a vessel rides trim and with its deck level.

Fathom: Six feet.

Forecastle: The forward part of a vessel, under the deck, where the sailors live.

Foremast: The forward mast of a vessel.

Foul: The opposite of clear; entangled.

Free: A vessel running before a fair wind at its stern.

Freeboard: The side of a vessel's hull that is out of the water.

Furl: To roll a sail up snugly on a yard or boom.

Gaff: A spar to which the head of a fore-and-aft sail is bent.

Gaff-Topsail: A light sail set over a gaff.

Galley: The place on a vessel where meals are prepared.

Gunwale: The upper rail of a boat or vessel.

Halyards: Ropes or tackles used for hoisting and lowering yards, gaffs and sails.

Hatch: An opening in the deck through which cargo is raised and lowered.

Hawse-Hole: The hole in the bows through which the anchor cable runs.

Hawser: A heavy rope or cable.

Head Sails: Sails set forward of the foremast.

*Sailors at work on the deck of the schooner-barge **Abissinia**. The vessel wrecked on Lake Erie in 1917. Courtesy Institute for Great Lakes Research.*

Heave-To: Stopping a vessel.

Helm: The machinery by which a vessel is steered.

Hogged: A vessel that droops at the ends.

Hold: The interior of a vessel's hull where cargo is stored.

Hull: The body of a vessel.

Irons: When a ship is in irons it cannot be steered one way or the other.

Jack-block: A block used in sending topgallant masts up and down.

Jacob's Ladder: A ladder made with ropes with wood steps used for boarding vessels.

Jib: A triangular sail mounted forward.

Jib Boom: The boom mounted beyond the bowsprint to which the tack of the jib sail is lashed.

Jury-mast: A temporary mast, rigged at sea, to replace one that is lost.

Keel: The main timber running the length of a vessel and supporting the frame.

Keelson: A timber placed over the keel of a vessel, located above the floor.

Labor: A vessel is in labor when it is pitching and rolling in a storm.

Lanyards: Ropes passed through dead eyes for setting up rigging.

Lead: A piece of lead with a hole in it and a line attached, used for depth sounding.

Lee: The side away from the wind.

Lighter: A craft used in loading and unloading vessels.

List: The tipping of a vessel toward one side or another. A vessel that is out of balance.

Log-book: A journal kept by the chief officer reporting the travels and events on a vessel at sea.

Luff: To turn the vessel to take better advantage of the wind.

Lurch: The sudden rolling of a vessel to one side.

Mast: A spar mounted upright from the deck that supports the rigging, yards and sails.

Master: The commander of a vessel. The captain.

Mate: The officer ranking next to the master.

Midships: The timbers at the broadest part of a vessel.

Mizzen-mast: The after most mast of a ship.

Mooring: The fixing of a vessel to one location.

Oakum: A mixture of rope yarns and tar used for caulking vessels.

Painter: A rope attached to a bow of a boat to make it fast.

Pay-off: When a vessel's head falls off from the wind.

Port: The left side of a vessel as you look forward.

Quarter: The part of a vessel's side between the after part of the main chains and the stern.

Quarter deck: That part of the upper deck behind the mainmast.

Rail: Top of the bulwarks.

Ratlines: Lines running across the shrouds and used like a ladder in going aloft.

Reef: To take in sail. Also a ridge of rock or sand close to the surface of the water.

Rigging: A general term for all of the ropes of a vessel

Rudder: The steering device at the stern of a vessel.

Scuppers: Holes through which water runs from the deck.

Scuttle: A hole cut in the deck of a vessel for use as a doorway. Also a hole cut in the hull to make a vessel sink.

Sea: Waves caused by wind.

Seams: The space between blanks in a vessel's hull or deck.

Sheets: Ropes used in working a sail.

Shrouds: Ropes on each side of a vessel that support the masts.

Spars: A general term for masts, yards, booms and gaffs.

Sprit: A small sail or gaff used in smaller vessels.

Stanchions: Upright posts that support the beams of a vessel. Also the upright posts that support the bulwarks and rail.

Starboard: The right side of a vessel when looking forward.

Stays: Supporting ropes leading between masts.

Staysail: A triangular for-and-aft sail set from a stay.

Stem: The forward timber reaching from the keel to the bowsprit.

Stern: The after end of a vessel.

Stern-post: A timber at the extreme after end of a vessel reaching from the keel to the deck. The rudder is attached to the stern-post.

Stern-sheets: The after end of a boat, behind the rowers, where the passengers sit.

Surf: The breaking of a sea upon the shore.

Tack: To work a vessel against the wind by special use of the sails and running on angles first to starboard, then to port.

Taffrail: The rail at a ship's stern.

Tar: a liquid gum, from pine or fir trees, used for caulking and making ropes.

Topmast: The second mast, mounted on top of the mast rising from the deck.

Topsail: The second sail above the deck.

Topgallant sail: The third sail above the deck.

Tow: To pull one vessel behind another.

Trysail: A fore-and-aft sail set with a boom and gaff mounted on a small mast behind a lower mast.

Warp: To move a vessel with the aid of a rope made fast to a fixed object.

Way: Movement of a vessel through the water.

Wear: To change tack.

Weigh: To lift up, such as to weigh anchor.

Wheel: The steering instrument of a vessel.

Winch: Purchase with the aid of a rope wound around a horizontal spindle or shaft with a wheel or crank at one end.

Windlass: The machine used to weigh anchor.

About the Author

James L. Donahue was born June 1, 1938 at Harbor Beach, Michigan. He discovered an interest in writing in high school and took a part-time job on the *Harbor Beach Times.* While in college, Donahue took a year off from his studies to work for the *Huron Daily Tribune,* Bad Axe, Michigan. Following graduation from Central Michigan University with majors in Journalism and English literature, Donahue went to work for the former *News-Palladium* in Benton Harbor, Michigan. He later worked two years at the *Kalamazoo Gazette,* Kalamazoo, Michigan, and finally became Sanilac County bureau chief for the *Times Herald,* Port Huron, Michigan, in 1971. He retired in 1993 to found Anchor Publications, a family-owned publishing business involved in literary and historical writing and research.

Donahue writes a syndicated weekly column for the *Times Herald,* the *Mining Journal,* Marquette, Mich., and the *Huron Daily Tribune,* Bad Axe, Mich., about shipwrecks and other historical events on the lakes. His stories also have appeared in the *Grand Rapids Press* and the *Traverse City Record Eagle.* In 1991, Donahue included seventy-five of his best stories in a collection titled *Terrifying Steamboat Stories,* published by Altwerger & Mandel Publishing Co.

Donahue collaborated with Judge James H. Lincoln, Harbor Beach, Michigan, in the book *Fiery Trial,* a historical account of a forest fire that swept the Thumb Area of Michigan in 1881. *Fiery Trial* was published by the Historical Society of Michigan in 1984. Anchor Publications reprinted a revised form of *Fiery Trial,* with the cooperation of the Historical Society, in 1994. In 1982, Donahue and his wife, Doris, owned and used an old-time wood-burning cook stove in their home. They wrote and published *Cooking On Iron,* a collection of early American recipes ranging from Chestnut Soup and Hickory Nut Cake, to making soap. His story, *The Day We Wrecked the Train,* a personal account about growing up in Harbor Beach, appeared in a special edition of *Good Old Days Magazine* in 1987.

Donahue also wrote and published *Steaming Through Smoke and Fire 1871.* The book, self-published in 1990, is a collection of true stories about shipwrecks and other events affecting vessels on the Great Lakes during the year 1871. Also look for *Steamboats in Ice 1872,* expected to be published in 1995.

James and Doris Donahue live near Cass City, Mich., with their daughter, Jennifer. The Donahues have three other children; Aaron, who lives with his wife, Gayle, in California, Ayn Bishop, of Georgia, and Susie Donahue, who lives in Germany.